All rights reserved. In accordance with the U.S. Copyright Act of 1976, the scanning, uploading, and electronic sharing of any part of this book without permission of the publisher is unlawful piracy and theft of the author's intellectual property. If you would like to use material from the book (other than for review purposes), prior written permission must be obtained by contacting the publisher at info@thedevangroup.com.

****

Scripture quotations are taken from the "THE HOLY BIBLE, NEW INTERNATIONAL VERSION Copyright (C) 1973, 1978, 1984, 2011 BY BIBLICA, Inc. Used with Permission. All rights reserved worldwide."

Library of Congress Control Number: 2025943042

Published by the DeVan Group Publishing
• Bowie, Maryland ISBN: 978-1-64589-071-3
Copyright © 2025 The DeVan Group

Printed in the United States of America

A Journey to Purpose
How to Cultivate a Dynamic Relationship with God

BY

RICK MCDONALD

"We want to tell you about the One who was from the beginning. We have seen Him with our own eyes, heard Him with our own ears, and touched Him with our own hands. This One is the manifestation of the life-giving Voice, and He showed us real life, eternal life.

We have seen it all, and we can't keep what we witnessed quiet—and so we have to share it with you now- before another goes by. And we are inviting you to experience this eternal life through the One who was with the Father and came down to us. "
- John the Beloved

"The Son is the radiance of God's glory and the exact representation of his being, sustaining all things by his powerful word"
(Hebrews 1:3).

CONTENTS

- *Forward*..3
- *Preface*...5
- *Introduction*..10

✦ Chapter 1
The Battle for Identity..13

✦ Chapter 2
The Groaning..20

✦ Chapter 3
Eternity in the Heart: Finding God's Purpose..........25

✦ Chapter 4
Cultivating a Dynamic Relationship with God........32

✦ Chapter 5
The Highest Expression of Love: Saying Yes to God..............39

✦ Chapter 6
Finding God in Solitude..46

✦ Chapter 7
His Timing: Learning to Move with God.................53

✦ Chapter 8
The Seasons that Shape Us.......................................63

✦ Chapter 9
The Opposition that Sharpens Us............................70

Chapter 10
Be Still..76

Chapter 11
The Battle for Hearts and Minds...............................84

Chapter 12
The Volunteers..97

Chapter 13
The Nature and Character of God............................108

Chapter 14
Let God Do It...118

Conclusion
The Journey Continues...123

FOREWORD

✦ I have known Rick McDonald for most of his adult life—since his teenage years until now—and I have watched him grow in faith and in his pursuit of an intimate walk with God. Over the years, I've been deeply impressed by his willingness to be an instrument of the Lord, wherever and whenever the call to ministry arose. Whether in Hungary, Africa, Ukraine, Israel, Hawaii, or in troubled cities across America, Rick not only accepted the challenge but stepped forward to exalt Jesus and bring change wherever the opportunity appeared.

Rick truly embodies the title Journey to Purpose. His life reflects the very message he shares here, blending personal experience with the hard-won knowledge of the Lord gained through decades of service. This book is both uplifting and challenging, inviting every reader to cultivate a dynamic relationship with God. I am proud of Rick as he bears his soul and his story for a generation that needs the hope and power of Christ.

Pastor Terry Kirk
Emeritus and Founding Pastor
Central Christian Assembly,
Baltimore, Maryland

✦ I have known Rick McDonald for 30 years, and he delivers this book with unmistakable passion, giving readers the nuts and bolts of ministry and the Christian life while lifting the conversation to a higher level. He lays out the realities of spiritual challenges with clarity and honesty, showing how the unseen and the everyday meet, and he demonstrates through his own life that perseverance and obedience open the way for God's work.

Pastor Dominic Correlli
Pastor Perry Hall Family Worship Center
Perry Hall, Maryland

PREFACE

"Therefore I tell you, do not worry about your life..."
(Matthew 6:25).

I still remember the moment I first encountered the Holy Spirit as a person. As the man who led me to Christ (Ken Freebairn) and I talked in his office one day, there was a sudden shift in the room, as if someone invisible just walked into the office, emanating peace and safety.

Then came this holy hush over me and the office space. This presence was weighty. Ken didn't even look up from his work as he spoke: "Rick, meet the Holy Spirit. Holy Spirit, meet Rick."

The next thing I knew, I was face down on the ground, completely overwhelmed by the weight of God's presence. Within seconds, I was being delivered from dark things I didn't even realize were holding me back. I lay on that ground as if time didn't exist. We weren't even talking about anything spiritual. I had just come over to his house after church.

I was 26 years old and had given my life to Jesus just two weeks earlier, and immediately God was moving on me with fire. All those years of running after the world and all those lonely nights were over with just one touch from Jesus and His Holy Spirit.

I was so new and so freshly saved, and I kept worrying: How could I keep it going? What is my calling? What is my purpose? How can I do this or that? I was filled with a thousand questions. Who am I? What am I? Where do I get more? How do I do this?

Thank God for the mentors and fathers God set me up with—they are all still here decades later. Listen, God is the same yesterday, today, and forever, and He shows no favoritism. What He does for one, He will do for another. The Holy Spirit continues to move powerfully today. He is drawing men and women all over the planet to Jesus. And He is radically encountering the ones who are desperate and those who seem hopeless yet are hungry.

"Blessed are those who hunger and thirst for righteousness, for they will be filled." **(Matthew 5:6).**

From the very beginning, I encountered God's presence through dreams, out-of-body experiences with Him, and witnessing signs and wonders. Since my baptism in the Spirit, God has moved swiftly in my life. Yet, despite numerous encounters, I still yearned to know God more deeply.

The Holy Spirit was making Jesus real to me daily, and Jesus was showing up. He was the one who created all my future encounters by filling me with a hunger and curiosity to pursue Jesus with relentless devotion—a hunger that God created in me, which continues to grow 33 years later.

With intentional pursuit, curiosity will open doors, and delighting in God's presence only increases those desires and curiosity. It creates a godly cycle—a hunger that feeds itself. The more faithful we are with His Word and His encounters, the more He will keep showing up. Wherever He is invited, He comes, and where He is honored, He stays. We don't want just a visitation—we want a habitation. Jesus is not an event; He is a powerful river that ever flows.

The people we admire for their faith and anointing didn't

reach their current state by accident, chance, or time. Their pursuit of God was intentional. They sought Him deliberately, making Him the focus of their lives. They placed God at the center and sought Him with all their hearts, day and night. They took God at His word:

"Keep this Book of the Law always on your lips; meditate on it day and night, so that you may be careful to do everything written in it. Then you will be prosperous and successful." **(Joshua 1:8).**

Every time I read these verses, I envision Joshua as a young man sitting by a river, next to a tree, surrounded by a forest. Sitting there, pouring over the Word of God with angels next to him. And he is just sitting there reading and meditating on God's words as the Spirit and the Word wash over him.

That image shaped my heart as the foundation of my walk with God. I wanted to be like that image of Joshua out in the wilderness by the river, seeking God for hours. Later in his life, as his spiritual father and mentor, Moses, passed away, Joshua faced the monumental task of leading God's people into the Promised Land.

In this critical moment of transition, as a young man grew into a wise leader, God spoke directly to Joshua with instructions that remain profoundly relevant for anyone seeking a lasting, deep relationship with the Lord. God then laid out the formula for a prosperous and successful life for Joshua:

"Keep God's Word at the center of everything. Remember your mentor and his teaching. Don't turn to the left or right. Be strong and courageous and stay focused." **(Joshua 1:7).**

And then God promises Joshua:

"I will be with you wherever you go." **(Joshua 1:9).**

God is giving Joshua a blueprint for success—a promise with a condition: Keep My Word, remember your teachings, be strong and courageous as you lead men and women. This means don't have a fear of man while obeying my commands. Be intentional with devotion to study and a passion for His presence above all else.

What worked for young Joshua will work for you, as he grew up under Moses; he went from a young, devoted follower to an older, wiser national leader. All along the way, he developed a relentless and intentional pursuit of God. And you can't go wrong either. You want to do great things for God? Do you want to make a difference in the world with Christ?

Keep God's Word at the center of your life, devote yourself to His presence, and He will instill a hunger in you to know Him more and more, and you will be filled to overflowing.

"...those who hunger and thirst will be filled!" **(Matthew 5:6).**

This is how we cultivate a deep, dynamic relationship with God. By being desperate for His attention and His love, and not worrying about anything else in this world, for God provides it all.

> The power is in the pursuit.
> Let's enjoy this wild ride together!

INTRODUCTION:
A FIELD GUIDE FOR THE BURNING ONES

I wrote this book to be a field guide to the greatest adventure and relationship you will ever experience—a life lived in intimate relationship with God and with Godly purpose. This book is a road map. It's a call to return to the heart of God. To trust His timing. To live for more than this world and oneself.

Whether you are weary, lost, or rooted deep in faith, this is an invitation to draw closer to God—to step into His fullness and embrace your created purpose. You are not alone; you were created for the greatest purpose of all. To know God, be known by Him, and then to make Him known.

You may feel that no one is making room for you while you're burning in your heart for more of God and for your purpose to be revealed. Yet I have incredible news for you - God is making room for you now in this generation. Now is your time to step out from the shadows and into the fire of God and his divine calling for you- and to do so fearlessly. Because You are a Burning One and God has a mission and purpose just for you on the road ahead.

"Did not our hearts burn within us while He talked with us on the road?" **(Luke 24:32).**

DEDICATION

Dedicated to Jesus Christ and His Burning Ones,
and to my family and my friends.

*They triumphed over him by the blood of the Lamb
and by the word of their testimony; they did not love
their lives so much as to shrink from death*
(Revelation 12:10).

CHAPTER 1
THE BATTLE FOR IDENTITY

*"The earth is the Lord's, and everything in it.
The world and all its people belong to him"*
(Psalm 24:1).

The world is shaking right now. It's groaning under the weight of sin and the oppression that comes with it. But hear me—it's not dying. Yet it struggles, straining under the weight of evil, waiting—longing—for this generation to rise and bring heaven to earth, bringing its deliverance. As the apostle Paul said:

"For the creation waits in eager expectation for the children of God to be revealed... We know that the whole creation has been groaning as in the pains of childbirth right up to the present time" **(Romans 8:19, 22).**

Creation is waiting for the children of God to appear—full of faith, full of glory, full of passion, strength, and courage. For too long, we've allowed the enemy to strip generations of their God-breathed identities.

We've watched as darkness has blurred the lines, confusing hearts and minds about the most fundamental truths of who we are. The battle for our identity rages fiercer than ever before. But I'm here to tell you—this is precisely the moment you were created for.

This is the moment we will see a significant multi-generational pushback against the lies and false propaganda of Lucifer. A generation of reformers is here. For in every generation, God planted reformers and disruptors like Gideon, Josiah, Paul, and of course, Jesus.

I believe you are one of them - one of God's disruptors, one of His reformers. There are hundreds of ways to make a difference for Christ in your current world. Showing up where God wants you and following his lead is the first step. Come to God right now, wherever you are, and present yourself in prayer as an offering, a surrendered person. Before time began, your name was written in the halls of heaven.

This grace was given to us in Christ Jesus before the beginning of time." **(2 Timothy 1:9).**

"Before I formed you in the womb I knew you, before you were born I set you apart; I appointed you as a prophet to the nations" **(Jeremiah 1:5).**

Your identity wasn't meant to be created through self-help books or social media filters. No! It was meant to be discovered in the presence of God.

Your original design and purpose were ingrained in your DNA by the very hand of God. Then it is found and uncovered layer by layer in the presence of your Creator.

"... 'You are the God who sees me,' for she said, 'I have now seen the One who sees me.'" **(Genesis 16:13).**

He is "El Roi, "the God who sees you, the God who knows you, and now He is the God who calls you.

"Then I heard the voice of the Lord saying, 'Whom shall I send? And who will go for us?' And I said, 'Here am I. Send me!' **(Isaiah 6:8).**

As usual, the enemy is doing everything he can to deceive people about God, ourselves, and others, and to drag us away from truth and goodness. Every day, more people are being saved and filled to overflowing with God's presence, yet many are still deceived—abandoning reason, common sense, and righteousness. We are in the middle of an all-out battle between light and darkness. But praise God, there is so much hope because Christ is real and alive and close to the brokenhearted.

I truly believe that the greatest gift God has ever given mankind was a broken and empty heart. So, at the perfect time, each one of us would get so tired of trying to endlessly fill that void with this world. That we finally give up and turn to God, the one who made the void in us so that we would seek him. He created us, but sin broke us, and the goodness of God created a God shaped hole in us that only he could fill.

Throughout history, there's been a cry from heaven and a groan from the earth—both waiting for someone to step into the gap. The Lord is looking. The world is aching. And heaven is still searching for those bold enough to rise and stand in that sacred space between heaven and earth—to make a mark for God.

In every generation, God calls. In every era of darkness, God looks for light-bearers. And now, in our time, Jesus is calling again.

> *"I looked for someone among them who would build up the wall and stand before me in the gap on behalf of the land..."*
> **(Ezekiel 22:30).**

Daily, He cries out—looking for anyone who will hear, who will answer, who will step into the night carrying the blazing light of His love and power. He is the true Lion—the Lion of Judah—who walks the earth, roaring with holy authority, calling His friends, His tribe, His people to rise and run with Him.

"The LORD roars from Zion and thunders from Jerusalem..."
(Joel 3:16).

He is gathering His sons and daughters to move with Him to bring salvation to the lost, healing to the broken, and awakening to the nations. He's calling you. And He's looking for FRIENDS. He's summoning a remnant—those marked by fire, unshaken by fear, and unwilling to settle for anything less than revival.

This is a holy summons—a moment of consecration, a moment of commissioning. We are living in a time when the line between good and evil, light and dark, is no longer blurry. It's bold. It's blazing. And it's clear.

A time where Satan, through his proxies, has been stripping whole generations of their identities, of their genders, of their souls. The battle has been and is for the hearts and minds of everyone on earth. The battle for the minds of men is not conventional. It's asymmetrical, relentless, and waged in unseen realms.

It's not fought with tanks or drones—but with truth, prayer, and Spirit-filled lives laid down in surrender and fire.

God is raising up a radical breed of warriors: Spirit-led, unconventional, and forged in a secret place. They are desperate for more of God. They are furious about what has been stolen from them and their friends and families. They are bent on His return, and they are after the spoils of spiritual warfare.

These are the new front-line force multipliers—men and women desperate enough to be the tip of the spear. They move with holy resilience. They serve with a 24/7,

360-degree vision—always on mission, always burning with passion. They're not looking to blend in; they're born to stand out. Their assignment? To take the fight to the darkness, to win hearts, minds, and eternal souls for Jesus Christ.

Even now, God's light is shining. A sleeping generation is awakening. Hearts are becoming hungry. Revival trembles just beneath the surface. And those who've never darkened the doors of a church? They're starting to feel it.

Something's shifting. The darkness is being exposed. He is being revealed. And you—yes, you—are hearing it too. You're seeing it. You're feeling the ache. You're groaning inside, just like creation has been groaning. Your insides feel like they're going to burst. And you're praying: "God... there must be more." Friend, that groaning inside you? That's not restlessness. That's the Holy Spirit moving within you. That's God's invitation, calling you into something deeper, real, and alive.

"Deep calls are too deep in the roar of Your waterfalls..."
(Psalm 42:7).

God is calling you to engage, to move, to rise—and I'm here as a witness to that fact. I've seen it. I feel it too. God is at work in your life and our day. And the time is now. So, I ask you plainly: What are you going to do about the hunger inside you right now? Will you feed your flesh and move on with your everyday life, or will you take the red pill like Neo and answer the call to the higher plains with your Captain?

I say get up, say YES to GOD, and step into your ordained time right now. Pursue God with all your heart and soul with reckless abandon.

Time is short, friend. Let's go.

CHAPTER 2
THE GROANING

"And we believers also groan, even though we have the Holy Spirit within us as a foretaste of future glory, for we long for our bodies to be released from sin and suffering. We too wait with eager hope for the day when God will give us our full rights as His adopted children, including the new bodies He has promised us"
(Romans 8:23).

The groaning you sense in your spirit is not just an ordinary longing—it is your spirit crying out to be clothed with heaven and your new body. It feels the weight of this world and longs for a time when sin will no longer dominate over creation.

This deep yearning is the Holy Spirit within you, groaning for more of God, more of His presence, more of His purposes, and more of heaven. It's an inward craving that you might not always recognize at first, and when you're unsure of what it is, you might try to satisfy it with things like food, exercise, or other activities. These may offer temporary relief, but the groaning rises again.

Eventually, you realize that what you truly crave is a deeper connection with God—a connection that only He can satisfy. This is not a hunger that can be filled by earthly means. It is a spiritual hunger that can only be fulfilled through His Word, prayer, and communion with Jesus.

The Holy Spirit is urging you to pause what you're doing, step away from distractions, and connect with God. It's a call to pray in the Spirit and to pray consistently. This is how we grow a dynamic relationship with God through intimacy with God—by nurturing the relationship that He longs for with us.

"And the Holy Spirit helps us in our weakness. For example, we don't know what God wants us to pray for. But the Holy Spirit prays for us with groanings that cannot be expressed in words" **(Romans 8:26).**

The more you know Him, the more you want Him. The

more you seek Him, the more you will find Him. You can search through the Word and ask in prayer, but when it's time to knock, you must be close and personal with God. That deep longing or groaning you feel? It's God's Spirit working inside you—drawing you toward Him, stirring your heart to pursue Him.

Do you understand that? God Himself causes us to desire Him. The passion is in the pursuit. It's found in prayer, in communion, in the desperate hunger that rises within you, making you want more of God, more of His presence, more of His Word in you.

That is the work of the Holy Spirit, causing many to feel an emptiness and a desperation for change—and that's what revival is, right? Revival is a soul hungry and desperate for transformation, not just in behavior but in being. A radical shift. It's God calling you to come home, to return, or to draw near to where He is. If we are hungry for God, we will move out from where we are to find out where He is. We won't stay stagnant; we will move.

It will be the work of the Holy Spirit within, causing us to get up and move, to change, and to pursue God. He is the one who is stirring in us and the work in us. It is the work of the Spirit of God that causes us to hunger for Him and to move toward where He is. He will lead you to other people who are hungry for God. He will help assemble people around you who are like-minded and are willing to go the extra mile with you on this journey to purpose.

So, what do we do after we come to Jesus? We don't stop there—we pursue His heart passionately. We seek Him for wisdom, knowledge, love, healing, and restoration—and above all, we seek His friendship.

How? Daily, no matter how you feel—and you won't always feel it or sense you're even close—but push through and bang on the door of God's heart and scream if you have to: "LET ME IN!"

"...everyone who seeks finds. And to everyone who knocks, the door will be opened" **(Matthew 7:7-8).**

I mean, if you meet someone and you're falling hard for them, one kiss isn't enough. You want the whole package, and you want it for life. You want the entire field, not just the shiny pearl in the middle. You're ready to give everything to have it all.

"The Kingdom of Heaven is like a treasure that a man discovered hidden in a field. In his excitement, he hid it again and sold everything he owned to get enough money to buy the field" **(Matthew 13:44).**

You'll overpay because true love requires a response, and our daily pursuit of God is our way of cultivating our hearts and our lives as soil for the seeds of God's Word, His promises, and His revelations.

We want to pursue God with a holy, righteous purpose that borders on recklessness and fiery passion. I'm serious —when we open our hearts more and more to God, we will burn with desire for Him. And the more we burn, the more we will earnestly seek His heart, His mind, and His presence.

I promise you this—if you choose to go down this road,

this narrow road, nothing else will ever satisfy you. Nothing in this world will ever again fulfill your soul or your being like the love, the power, and the overwhelming presence of God. Once you've tasted Jesus and His love, everything else pales in comparison.

Nothing compares. Nothing even comes close. Yet, like anything in our lives, we have a responsibility to cultivate this relationship with God. And we will be empowered from within by Christ in us, so that He will lead us from faith to faith and from glory to glory.

"And we all, who with unveiled faces contemplate the Lord's glory, are being transformed into his image with ever-increasing glory, which comes from the Lord, who is the Spirit" **(2 Corinthians 3:18).**

We will face many trials and tests along the way, but they all will prove to be tools in the hands of God in the process of sanctification as God cleans us up, builds us, and equips us for the works of Jesus and the life of the same.

"Consider it pure joy, my brothers and sisters, whenever you face trials of many kinds, because you know that the testing of your faith produces perseverance. Let perseverance finish its work so that you may be mature and complete, not lacking anything" **(James 1:2-4).**

CHAPTER 3
ETERNITY IN THE HEART: FINDING GOD'S PURPOSE

*"He has made everything beautiful in its time.
He has also set eternity in the human heart;
yet no one can fathom what God
has done from beginning to end"*
(Ecclesiastes 3:11).

All I ever wanted as a kid was to live a full, adventurous life — even though I didn't fully understand what that meant at the time. Much of my early life was spent in a state of survival, constantly reacting to and adjusting to my surroundings. Like many, I was born into a world I didn't choose and planted in soil I didn't pick. This is probably the experience of many, if not all, of us.

We are born into a world we do not know, and we start growing in the soil into which we were planted. For a high percentage of people, that soil was fertile, and that garden was fruitful. Yet, there are so many around the globe who were born into difficult, sometimes horrible, conditions and situations. We then spend the next decades learning to cope and survive.

We are all born into this world the same way, but the process is different for each of us. At some point, we are shaped by genetics and environment, facing difficulties and challenges that will break us, make us, or help us grow as we adapt. As Jesus reminded us,

"In this world you will have trouble. But take heart! I have overcome the world" **(John 16:33).**

I was born somewhere between bad and challenging. Life felt like a field of landmines. I was always trying to dodge what could blow up. It was like I came through the birth canal leading to the hospital, out into a world that was, well, basically "welcome to the jungle, let's get started..."

For me, it became a life of needing constant stimulation of seeking adventure, action, escaping, and dreaming, playing, and absorbing knowledge from all the human sources I could. I became Hyper-vigilant and was Hyperactive. I had to learn how to read the room, the street, and the world around me to understand who was who and what was what. All the while, finding myself withdrawn for hours and days at a time, reading everything I could and then going out to roam the neighborhood with insane high-octane energy. To meet and connect with people and to learn about life as fast as I could.

Life was a roller coaster—bursts of energy, fits of rage, wild highs, and crushing lows. I dreamed daily, and I wanted to experience everything at once. I chased knowledge, adventure, and escape. The result was a world full of ups and downs, a desire to run away and touch, feel, and see everything I could—my mind filled with dreams and escapism.

Yet all of this was fueled by a profound sense of brokenness, loneliness, and rejection. The pain that filled my heart as a child and teen was profound enough that my acting out had my family and friends concerned for years. My environment, the one in my home, was one of ups and downs and crashing lows and rising highs. We never knew what to expect, and the rejection inside caused all my wildness to come out.

There were many explosions of anger inside me that could be triggered at any moment—usually when I saw someone trying to hurt someone I loved or a bully. I would go "dark" fast. I never felt a sense of belonging unless I was high on something or playing sports—yet when the games and drugs wore off, there I was, alone, at least inside my head.

Yet, there was a feeling—a sense of something else inside me, another feeling that there was more... there was this presence surrounding my life I couldn't shake. There were seasons filled with confusion, isolation, and a restless search for meaning. Days passed in solitude, wandering through fields or spending hours alone—kicking a ball, swinging a golf club, or throwing rocks—seeking comfort or purpose in simple motion. Even then, there was an unseen presence, a stirring deep inside, guiding each step just enough to avoid disaster. Like a toddler learning to walk with unseen hands always near, there was divine protection shaping the journey.

"You hem me in behind and before, and you lay your hand upon me. Such knowledge is too wonderful for me, too lofty for me to attain" **(Psalm 139:5-6).**

Voices of doubt, rejection, and fear often filled the mind, yet another voice stirred from within—one whispering of purpose, destiny, and belonging. Despite missteps and brushes with danger, something sacred held firm, preserving life from collapse. That quiet voice was not imagined; it was the Spirit of God, patiently leading, preserving, and calling.

"Whether you turn to the right or to the left, your ears will hear a voice behind you, saying, 'This is the way; walk in it'" **(Isaiah 30:21).**

Although divine intervention wasn't always recognized, hindsight reveals a sustaining presence. Near-death moments, reckless decisions, and internal battles could have ended the story. But grace prevailed. The mercy of God, silent and steadfast, encircled every moment, even when misunderstood or ignored.

"The LORD will keep you from all harm—he will watch over your life; the LORD will watch over your coming and going both now and forevermore" **(Psalm 121:7-8).**

God's hands were present, holding and protecting, even in the solitude of childhood. Looking back, those lonely places weren't empty at all—they were filled with divine companionship. The voice that had been so subtle was, in truth, a constant call home.

Even when I didn't know Him, He knew me. Even when I wandered, he pursued me. Even when I rebelled, he stayed near. The ache was always His invitation to come home.

"I have loved you with an everlasting love; I have drawn you with unfailing kindness" **(Jeremiah 31:3).**

Over time, it became clear that what seemed like personal resilience was actually God's sustaining grace. A much deeper truth emerged: God was pursuing me from the beginning. "He...set eternity in the human heart..." This universal longing for God is not just one person's story. It is humanity's—the collective longing for God. The deep ache to belong and to know why we exist is answered in the heart of our Creator—God. Careers, relationships, and experiences cannot satisfy the ache meant to draw us back to Him. God created us with that longing to lead us home.

"God did this so that they would seek him and perhaps reach out for him and find him, though he is not far from any one of us" **(Acts 17:27).**

Psalm 139 speaks of being knit together in the womb, fearfully and wonderfully made.

"He has also set eternity in the human heart..." **(Ecclesiastes 3:11).**

This revelation reframes our stories. What once seemed random or futile becomes sacred. The detours and darkness weren't wasted; they were part of a divine pursuit. Redemption, then, is not just being saved—it's discovering that we've been known and loved all along.

"But God demonstrates his own love for us in this: While we were still sinners, Christ died for us" **(Romans 5:8).**

God's love transcends background, birth, and brokenness. His pursuit is personal—you're His son and His daughter, created in His image for good. His presence has always been near, even in the hidden and hurting places. He designed the ache in you for more so that we would ultimately find our way back to Him.

"I have loved you with an everlasting love; I have drawn you with unfailing kindness" **(Jeremiah 31:3).**

"Return to me, and I will return to you," says the LORD Almighty **(Malachi 3:7).**

The journey from rebellion to redemption is the same for all of us. God has always been both Rescuer and Companion. Even when ignored, He remains faithful. Even when misunderstood, He draws near. For some, it's a whisper. For others, a thunderous call. But for all, it is His invitation to return—to rediscover identity, purpose, and belonging in the One who never left. The story doesn't end at salvation. It continues as we respond to His love by seeking Him again. The same hands that protected us in childhood now invite us into friendship and mission.

This is the testimony: You were known. You were pursued. You were loved before you were conceived and blessed before you were born. And now, the journey continues—not just walking with God but running after Him. No matter where you stand today, His plan for you remains the same.

It was God all along. And it will still be Him chasing after me and you for much longer:

"And surely I am with you always, to the very end of the age" **(Matthew 28:20).**

He doesn't leave us alone—He sent His Son to take our place on the cross, and He sent His Spirit to teach us and show us the way forward.

"When the Spirit of truth comes, he will guide you into all the truth..." **(John 16:13).**

And He gives us so many great promises that are always proven true, and all you need to do now is pursue Him:

"Draw near to God and He will draw near to you" **(James 4:8).**

CHAPTER 4
CULTIVATING A DYNAMIC RELATIONSHIP WITH GOD

"For you created my inner being; you knit me together in my mother's womb"
(Psalm 139:13).

Building a dynamic relationship with God begins with cultivation—a consistent seeking after His heart, His mind, and His presence, for the sole purpose of becoming as close to Him as humanly possible.

What is my purpose? Why am I here? What can I do to help? Why, God?

These are the most valid questions a human being can have, and they are fair. Yet what if I told you that they were pre-placed and predesigned inside you before time was ever created?

"For he chose us in him before the creation of the world to be holy and blameless in his sight. In love" **(Ephesians 1:4).**

What if I told you that God created you to ask Him, "Why do I exist?" and "What is my purpose?"

That God placed that longing in your heart while you were being knit together by Him in your mother's womb, and that He placed that groaning, hunger, and those questions in you so that you would seek Him and find Him. We were created to have a living, breathing, life-changing, day-to-day, moment-to-moment dynamic relationship with God through Jesus Christ.

All your deepest desires, which beat within you for love and connection, adventure, and truth, all came from Him, and they can only be fulfilled by Him within you. In the following pages, I hope to have placed in your hands something that may inspire you to pursue God with absolute surrender.

Why should you pursue a vibrant relationship with God? Because that's the purpose for which we were created. That's the why and the what, and everything else will follow. Let's start by committing to knowing God as our life's goal, and He will make you His.

"But seek first his kingdom and his righteousness, and all these things will be given to you as well" **(Matthew 6:33).**

Everything with God follows this verse; it is the Matthew lifestyle. Seek God first, and all you will ever need will follow behind you. All we need is found in him first. He provides as we follow.

Fire prepares us for Glory.

"For the fire tests the vessel, but it does not consume it; it refines, purifies, and prepares the heart to carry His glory" **(Malachi 3:3) (paraphrased).**

We see the temple of God is refined by fire. There is judgment, repentance, and trouble—yet for the remnant who waited, God declares:

"Look! I am sending my messenger, and he will prepare the way before me. Then the Lord you are seeking will suddenly come to his Temple. The messenger of the covenant, whom you look for so eagerly, is surely coming," says the LORD of Heaven's Armies" **(Malachi 3:1).**

These are the ones who waited—those who spent time in the secret place, who gathered together to speak of Him, who sought His love and approval more than that of men. They sat together and talked about the Lord. They nurtured their relationship with Him. They sat in quiet places, prayed, studied His Word, and meditated on it day and night.

"But they delight in the law of the LORD, meditating on it day and night" **(Psalm 1:2).**

These are the ones who, after judgment came, were found to be the bride who made herself ready—the wise virgins who kept oil in their lamps.

"For the wedding of the Lamb has come, and his bride has made herself ready" **(Revelation 19:7).**

These are those who, in quiet desperation, prayed, studied, and drew closer to God. For even though in Him we live, move, and have our being, this closeness only creates a deeper desire to see Him, to know Him, to be with the One our hearts long for, the One our souls ache for. These are the ones who asked God, day and night, for the fire of God to come all over them. To be baptized in the fire. Who gave themselves as the offering at the altar and who kept seeking after God until they were filled to overflowing.

It is not the gifts that God gives men that will set people free; it's the anointing that breaks all the yokes of sin off people and nations. We need that anointing, that fire, and we need it now. We must be hungry and desperate for God in these hours so that we will climb the highest hills to get a hold of Jesus. We will push through the crowds to pull on His garments. It's the anointing that breaks the yoke and bondages of sin. Giftings fill stadiums full of people, but it is the anointing that will send them home free of their addictions.

"And it shall come to pass on that day, that his burden shall be taken away from off thy shoulder, and his yoke from off thy neck, and the yoke shall be destroyed because of the anointing" **(Isaiah 10:27).**

Why should I cultivate a "dynamic relationship with God"? Because that is what you were created for—to know God and for God to know you. That is the original design and operating system that God has placed inside of you. And these days, that is what will see you through all the trials, tests, and heartaches you will experience, as well as those of the people around you.

The reason you exist—the sole purpose—is to know God and to be one with Him through experience and faith, and to share that with the world and the culture you live in. We are not promised anything in this world that compares to the promises God has made to us in His Word: that those who seek Him will find Him, that those who pursue Him will have Him, and that He honors those who honor Him.

"Jesus replied, 'I am the bread of life. Whoever comes to me will never be hungry again. Whoever believes in me will never be thirsty" **(John 6:35).**

Living a life apart from God is not what you were made for, and in the same vein, living a life with God but not pursuing Him passionately is almost as empty. To come to Jesus, stop, and say, "That's enough, I am saved, I am good," and to forget the benefits that come with salvation is useless.

Jesus promised us that we could have life, and life abundantly—life and life plus, or the upgraded version of life. We can have a natural life and a supernatural life, a life in the Spirit and of the Spirit. As He said:

The thief's purpose is to steal and kill and destroy. My purpose is to give them a rich and abundant life" **(John 10:10).**

We are not called to merely exist; it's a life that transcends the natural, a life filled with purpose, power, and peace, in constant relationship with the Creator. If you want to have just enough Jesus and enjoy nice things, live a nice life, go ahead—that's fine.

But we are called to do more than exist, eat, sleep, work, and play. We are called to a profound and rich experience with God that transcends this world. The earth is not our destination; we will rule and reign with Him one day soon, and we will be known for who we really are. We don't just live our lives here; we are sowing seed for a millennial reign with Christ as the King in the center of the heavenly Jerusalem.

"Then I saw 'a new heaven and a new earth,' for the first heaven and the first earth had passed away, and there was no longer any sea. I saw the Holy City, the new Jerusalem, coming down out of heaven from God" **(Revelation 21:1-2).**

We must understand this is not just a practical life—it's life and life abundant. We are called to a much higher form of life and service. What we do now will be known to God forever.

"For we must all appear before the judgment seat of Christ, so that each of us may receive what is due us for the things done while in the body, whether good or bad" **(2 Corinthians 5:10).**

We must live life with eternity in full view of our everyday decisions and actions, for they will tell all creation who we really see as our Lord—Him or ourselves. There is no middle ground; you're either all in or not. The devil will keep coming at us, so it is better to get off the fence and into the battle.

"Be alert and of sober mind. Your enemy the devil prowls around like a roaring lion looking for someone to devour. Resist him, standing firm in the faith" **(1 Peter 5:8-9).**

I encourage you with these words: Christ will return soon, and it will be like a thief in the night. He will come, and he will be there suddenly. And those who are ready now will be ready then. So, get oil in your lamps—the anointing and the pure oil of the Lord—and get set on fire.

Stay in the encounters. Don't be in a hurry. God is not an event. He comes where He is honored and stays where He is loved.

CHAPTER 5
THE HIGHEST EXPRESSION OF LOVE: SAYING YES TO GOD

"Teach me your ways, O Lord, that I may live according to your truth! Grant me purity of heart, so that I may honor you"
(Psalm 86:11).

Saying yes to God before we even know the why is the highest expression of love and trust a person can show Him. It means giving our yes to anything God asks or requires of us. To worship God through the pain, to praise Him in the secret place, and to serve with obedience—even in the face of our fears.

"Trust in the LORD with all your heart and lean not on your own understanding; in all your ways submit to him, and he will make your paths straight" **(Proverbs 3:5-6).**

Having a deep desire to seek God, stay open to Him, and give Him our yes as much as we can creates a lasting "yes" in our spirit, even forming a "yes spirit" around us.

"Here I am! I stand at the door and knock. If anyone hears my voice and opens the door, I will come in and eat with that person, and they with me" **(Revelation 3:20).**

Not everyone desires this kind of life—a life dedicated to seeking God's heart. Pursuing God in the mystery and through the unknown. No, not everyone pursues that life, but it is available: the absolute surrender of our souls to God, the giving of our "yes" to Him as much as we can, so that even in our sleep, our spirit and our soul say, "Yes, God. Yes, here I am. Yes."

"Then I heard the voice of the Lord saying, 'Whom shall I send? And who will go for us?' And I said, 'Here am I. Send me! **(Isaiah 6:8).**

Walking with God in true devotion will set you apart from the pack and may mark you as one who thinks they are something special, or trying to be different, or "too heavenly minded to do any earthly good." All of that is

Satan trying to gaslight you and diminish your greatest passion in life—a passion to know God.

"Do not conform to the pattern of this world" **(Romans 12:2).**

We can never care more about people's opinions about walking with God than God's opinion, ever, not once. If God is drawing you away, get away. If God is speaking, then stop and listen, and say what He says to say or do what He says to do.

"Am I now trying to win the approval of human beings, or of God? Or am I trying to please people? If I were still trying to please people, I would not be a servant of Christ" **(Galatians 1:10).**

Becoming a Fool for God's Glory

"The fear of man will prove to be a snare, but whoever trusts in the Lord is kept safe" **(Proverbs 29:25).**

Anyone who desires to be used by God in their generation in any capacity will go through a series of life-changing encounters with Jesus, if they want them. But one thing that will be sacrificed above all else is your fear of what people think about you. That has to be killed immediately and layer by layer over time.

You cannot be fearful of what man can do to you or think of you above God. You will never be used by God in any meaningful way if you worry about what people think of you.

Be that guy, be that girl, who is willing to be a fool in the eyes of mankind for the glory of your God. Be that fool for God every time. Because I am here to tell you one thing loud and clear: God honors those who honor Him.

"Those who honor me I will honor, and those who despise me will be disdained" **(1 Samuel 2:30).**

"For the message of the cross is foolishness to those who are perishing, but to us who are being saved it is the power of God" **(1 Corinthians 1:18).**

We must live life with eternity in view, knowing that God's eyes are on us every moment. All of heaven is watching us, and I want to live in such a way on this side of eternity that I will not be ashamed when I see God on the other side of eternity.

"Therefore, since we are surrounded by such a great cloud of witnesses, let us throw off everything that hinders and the sin that so easily entangles. And let us run with perseverance the race marked out for us" **(Hebrews 12:1).**

There will be many moments in your walk with God that will bring you into conflict with the will of men. And your commitment to God will always be challenged by those with less desire than you.

"In fact, everyone who wants to live a godly life in Christ Jesus will be persecuted" **(2 Timothy 3:12).**

That will happen, but to live for an audience of one, to pursue that which pursues us to take hold of who has grabbed us, is worship. To lead a life that is set apart is the only way to live, as the Bible says:

"For many are called, but few are chosen" **(Matthew 22:14).**

Many of your friends, peers, and family members are called to come closer, and many are called to know God more deeply, but very few of them will endeavor to climb the hillside to reach Him. Very few will pursue Him into the fire to get to Him. Very few will go past the fish and loaves to where we must eat and drink of His flesh.

"Very truly I tell you, unless you eat the flesh of the Son of Man and drink his blood, you have no life in you" **(John 6:53).**

That will cost you, and the more you pursue Him, the more you will find Him; the more you find Him, the more you want Him. He is the bread of life, and it is His bread that feeds us. And the more we have of Him, the more we desire Him.

"I am the bread of life. Whoever comes to me will never go hungry, and whoever believes in me will never be thirsty" **(John 6:35).**

He is the well that never runs dry; a river that flows from the throne; he is the satisfaction of hunger that creates more hunger. When we start eating better and healthier whole foods and drinking more water, our bodies begin to crave it even more. When we establish healthy eating habits, our bodies respond because we are providing them with the food they were designed to have.

"On the last and greatest day of the festival, Jesus stood and said in a loud voice, 'Let anyone who is thirsty come to me and drink. Whoever believes in me, as Scripture has said, rivers of living water will flow from within them" **(John 7:37-38).**

The same is true with divine food or the body and blood of Christ—when we partake of Jesus daily, we crave more of Jesus daily. God placed these desires within us when He created us.

We need to understand that eternity was placed within us specifically to pursue the One who implanted that desire. The desire to seek and find God is the greatest gift God has ever given—a desire to know Him.

"You will seek me and find me when you seek me with all your heart" **(Jeremiah 29:13).**

That is the purpose of life: to know God and to be known by Him. And then to live with eternity in view, knowing that all heaven is watching us, all the saints (former sinners like we were) are watching us, cheering us on.

"Now this is eternal life: that they know you, the only true God, and Jesus Christ, whom you have sent" **(John 17:3).**

All of eternity sees us now, and God sees all as He is within us and outside us, in our time and outside of time simultaneously. Watching our every thought before it is born in our mind and in eternity before it becomes an action. He sees the beginning of our lives from the end of them.

"I am God, and there is none like me, declaring the end from the beginning and from ancient times things not yet done" **(Isaiah 46:9-10).**

Every word on my lips, God knew before time began. And we must live with the light of His gaze on us each day. He sees you; He knows you, and He loves you.

"Before a word is on my tongue you, LORD, know it completely" **(Psalm 139:4).**

To walk after God in such a way that we are no more—to have an excellent spirit like Caleb who was ready to enter the Promised Land when others turned back—is to finish the race well. It all starts with a yes. "Yes, God. Yes, Father."

"But because my servant Caleb has a different spirit and follows me wholeheartedly, I will bring him into the land he went to, and his descendants will inherit it" **(Numbers 14:24).**

"Not my will, but yours be done" **(Luke 22:42).**

Despite numerous encounters, I still yearn to know God. God created all my future encounters and moments with Jesus and is calling us to come find them. Experiencing Him deeply, whether in small or big moments, only increases the desire for more. As the saying goes, "Faithful in the little, ruler of more."

The more faithful we are with His Word and His encounters, the more He will keep showing up. Where invited, He goes—just as anyone would. Because God loves those who love and honor Him and make space for Him, I believe we receive this from Him.

CHAPTER 6
FINDING GOD AND HIS WILL IN SOLITUDE: GOD'S ETERNAL DESIGN

"We love because he first loved us"
(1 John 4:19).

How can I hear the Voice of God? How do I know the voice of God? Here in the solitude.

"You have said, 'Seek my face.' My heart says to you, 'Your face, Lord, do I seek'" **(Psalm 27:8).**

There is a hunger that will rise inside you at times, which can only be filled by spending time alone with God in a place that is personal for you and God. A place where He is trying to draw you out so He can reveal His heart, which is just for you.

That place of solitude and comfort where you can open your heart and be free. A place to come to meet with God and to talk with your Creator.

The one who designed you, the one who knit you together and breathed life into you. The one who knows your original story and design, the way you think, the way you feel, and the way you process everything.

It is a hunger that can never be replaced or satisfied by anything other than being alone with Him. This is not the same "groaning" of creation for God that was mentioned earlier. No, this is a "groaning" of God for His creation, not just "of" the creation.

This is God's Spirit in you moving around in you as an invitation to come away with Him.

"My beloved spoke and said to me, 'Arise, my darling, my beautiful one, come with me. See!'" **(Song of Songs 2:10).**

It is an invitation to come away and experience Him, to have Him share His heart and secrets with you. This is the secret place of secret places. This is your audience with a King and His love in you, lending His scepter to you as He did for Esther. Inviting you into His chamber, where we can connect with his heart, hear his voice, and receive his wisdom

This is where we grow deeper. This is where the river flows freely. The secret place of His presence. In a closet, a forest, or a hillside all your own. And it is God drawing you in, causing you to feel His hunger for you.

As a child, I found peace in the chaotic world I lived in by going to isolated places to play alone, to get away from the drama of my daily life. It was in those places—in closets, basements, or in fields behind my home—where I would go off and create worlds of my own.

There were days and weeks when I would go down to the basement at my grandfather's house, sit alone on the steps, and read his encyclopedias for hours. Turning page after page, absorbing all this information about the world, sitting there reading and reading, feeling myself. I can look back now and see that He was always alongside me, hiding with me, pulling me away to quiet and lonely places to play and, in one sense, to pray.

This is when we are acting out what we were called to by God, even before we were saved.

As soon as I was saved, I locked myself in closets as a new believer, with a pillow, a blanket, a legal pad of paper, pens, and my Bible. From that very first weekend, I had an unwavering desire to be alone—to seek God, pray, sing, read, and write. This would become the foundation that God laid for me, one that He would build on to this day.

A desire to get alone, study, pray, sing, write, connect, and dream with God. To learn His voice and see things from His perspective, to gain wisdom, direction, and discernment.

God rewarded me with those desires to seek His face. Even having such desires was a gift from Him to me—a gift to mankind. Hunger is the greatest gift ever given to us by God after Jesus' life.

It is what will cause us to get up and move, to seek God in the most trying times. It is the motivating force within you that will take you from cold to hot overnight. From complacency to white-hot pursuit.

"The LORD himself goes before you and will be with you; he will never leave you nor forsake you. Do not be afraid; do not be discouraged" **(Deuteronomy 31:8).**

He instilled in us a strong desire to understand who we are, who we are meant to be, and the questions of "why are we here,' so that we would search for the answers—in reality, to seek after Him. He never intended for us to be alone, or robotic, but relational, so He put a homing beacon inside of us. That way, when we were ready, we would begin to seek Him out, to seek our purpose and our reason for being.

"We love because he first loved us" **(1 John 4:19).**

All those years of me seeking solitude in the dark places were actually God seeking after me and causing me to respond to and pursue Him. This dynamic relationship —God's pursuit and my response—created a sacred dance that continues to this day, each of us moving in perfect rhythm.

"Come, all you who are thirsty, come to the waters; and you who have no money, come, buy and eat! Come, buy wine and milk without money and without cost" **(Isaiah 55:1).**

Throughout the Bible, we see God as the initiator of everything with us. He is the one who initiates all contact, and He is the one who sent His Son to us. He loved us first. Jesus went about calling each of the disciples whom God the Father showed Him, and He called to all of them, saying,

"Come to me..."

The desire to seek God comes from God. The burning in your spirit to know God and to do exploits for God—they come from God. All these desires come from God, and you're just responding back to Him.

All that is good in our lives comes from God, and all the love you feel for God and for people comes from God, as we love God only because He first loved us.

You seek God because He placed that desire in you. He won't force you, but He gave you all the desires and ability to seek and find Him—and that's another form of worship. Worship is our response to His almightiness; it is us shouting, "You are WORTHY of it all."

Worship is our response to God, who is worthy, alive, present, and good. Worship is a response to God's invitation to seek Him. Worship is our response to the revelation that God was there, is here now, and God will always be.

Worship is reading the Word, working hard at your job, giving, singing, and living rightly—it all shows the world who we live for. That is worth-ship, and that is part of the blueprint to success.

The Solitude—The Word—The Prayers—all in the secret place between you and our Abba God, our Father who is worthy of every breath He gives us to take. So, all the questions you may have about your life, your future, eternity, or your purpose and calling—these all come from God. He is the one who works for us to seek Him and know Him.

He is the one who places the questions we need to ask to the answers He already wants to give. And they are all found in the solitude with God, meditating on His Word, connecting and learning His heart for you. All you need to do is respond to Him.

Love requires a response. All this hunger, these desires, and desperation are not just from you for God. It is also God inviting you into something very special. His hunger and desire for your presence with Him. This is His invitation to come to Him and to be with Him and learn of Him.

"Again He took the Twelve aside and told them what was going to happen to Him" **(Mark 10:32).**

This is where His Glory is. This is where the river flows the deepest—this is the Secret Place of His presence and where God wants to reveal His heart. Where He will share His dreams and His plans and His secrets with you, His friend.

He is searching for those who will willingly come away with Him... just to be with Him, no big agenda meeting. No intercession or prayers, no work to do... no. Just to come away and to BE and so to become more like Him.

CHAPTER 7
HIS TIMING: LEARNING TO MOVE WITH GOD

"For those who are led by the Spirit of God are the children of God"
(Romans 8:14).

We're not just called to work for God — we're called to walk with Him. Those whom the Spirit of God leads are His sons and daughters. That means we need to stay alert and in tune with the Holy Spirit within us. At any moment during the day, God may be pointing us in a certain direction, leading us to act, or asking us to respond — and we must be willing to move with Him.

One of the biggest things that holds people back is fear—fear of the unknown, fear of what might happen or not happen. Fear keeps us from testing the waters of life and robs us of rich experiences.

Yes, playing it safe might keep you from embarrassment, pain, or failure—but it will also keep you from experiencing beauty. Those afraid to love may never know its grandeur. Those afraid to grow often never do. Those afraid of God never come to understand His ways. Many times, God asks us to step out not to hurt us—but to free us. He wants to break the grip of fear. Most often, it's not about the action—it's about overcoming the fear that's holding us hostage.

"There is no fear in love, but perfect love drives out fear, because fear expects punishment. The person who is afraid has not been made perfect in love" **(1 John 4:18).**

God wants His children to be free from fear of man, fear of failure, and fear of the unknown. Deep down, many people truly desire that freedom. God sees that desire, and He responds to it. He may ask us to do something that seems small: give money we don't feel we have, pray out loud, walk to the altar, speak up, step out. But when we recoil, we're not just shrinking back from the moment —

we're pulling back from Him. We show we're more concerned about being hurt than hurting God's heart. More worried about survival than walking in His grace.

Here's the truth: God will not lead you to harm you. He leads you to set you free, to show you that He can be trusted. The more we move with God, the more we can move for God. We become partners—co-laborers with Him in doing great things. Being led inwardly by God to act is a sign of trust—not just in God's power, but in His character. We trust He'll keep us, protect us, love us, and provide for us.

Let me paint you a picture: You have a meeting scheduled at 11 a.m. on Tuesday. But around 10:15, you feel a tug—a prompting—to go somewhere else. Now, if you're just learning how to walk with God, you might think, "But Lord, I have a meeting. You're a God of order, and I want to keep my word." But the feeling persists. At 10:25, it's still there. You wrestle with it. I've been there many times. Sometimes I obey, and sometimes I don't.

One time, I chose to obey. I turned to go in the direction God was prompting—and just then, my phone rang. The 11 a.m. meeting was canceled. And I had the joy of stepping right into something else God had arranged. Other times, I ignored the prompting, drove to the meeting, and was stood up. The person canceled at the last minute. And I missed what God had waiting on the other path.

In both cases, I learned. I learned to know God not just by the letter but through His Spirit. I've experienced many of these moments. What I've discovered is this: if God is leading, He will give a peaceful prompting. What He asks of us is obedience.

And through these small acts of obedience, we learn that we can trust His leading—and even trust ourselves to hear correctly. He's preparing us for victory, not failure.

Remember: there are three people involved in every schedule—you, them, and God. And only one of you knows everything. So, we make our plans, pray, and listen. God knows that next Tuesday, Tom and his team will need to reschedule. He knows why. He knows when. You don't.

Both you and Tom might be excited to meet, to do this deal, to pray together. You're nervous. There's pressure. But God starts nudging you—Call Tom. Go here instead. And you're uneasy. You don't want to mess it up.

Then, Tom calls and cancels. And suddenly, you see it: God knew. But this time, maybe Tom was also nervous. Maybe God was working on his end, too, teaching him obedience, trust, and surrender.

You gave God your "yes," and now you're getting your "why." And you learn—wow—God had this all along.

God sets these moments up not just as tests, but as invitations to grow. To learn how to trust Him in the mystery, there is no growth without that trust.

God is always looking to set us up for a victory and even in the middle of obeying and following. He may lead us in a different direction, not always just sometimes. This expands our ability to trust and to do so in faith that he always leads us into encounters that will shape us and others.

It is sometimes an exercise to know Him better. To know His ways. He's not looking to disrupt your calendar for no reason—He's teaching you the dance of the Spirit. The rhythm of obedience. The joy of walking with Him. Yes, God values being on time, keeping your word, and showing up—but He wants to be first. When He's first, everything else falls into place. That's how we learn to move with God—not just for Him. These small, prophetic, practical moments are where His ways become real.

It teaches us that his guidance is trustworthy and that it is there to protect us. I have had dozens of encounters where God has seemingly overridden his own plans for me, only to discover his divine protection.

I can't tell you how many times God has "misdirected" me—on the way to doing what He had ultimately called me to do. And I either obeyed and was blessed—or disobeyed and was distressed. So, to you, my dearest young Jedi who is burning with a godly fire and passion...trust Him always.

There is a timing and a purpose to everything God has for us and places for us to be and not be.

"For there is a proper time and procedure for every matter, though a person may be weighed down by misery" **(Ecclesiastes 8:6).**

Timing affects quality. Some are called to build highways in the desert long before the world even knows that deserts exist. That is the work of prophetic seers, those who walk three to five years—or more—ahead of their time.

Vision and dreaming are crucial, but execution is what truly matters. You can have the most incredible vision, and everyone might be excited for you. However, it only takes one misstep in execution for that vision to be remembered less for its promise and more for its missteps.

You can have the most amazing product with an amazing vision attached to it, but you cannot sell what you cannot deliver. Your supply must be solid and intact, your path to market clear, and the market must be ready for your product.

You cannot introduce your beloved product into a market that isn't ready for it. Being a forerunner and a pioneer years ahead of others is a calling for some, but even then, a place has been made ready.

Being first to market can be an advantage—trailblazers set the stage. But sometimes, being second is even better. It allows you to observe, learn from others' mistakes, and avoid the pitfalls of moving too soon. Ultimately, though, the most important thing is not being first or second, but being on time—and the same principle applies to our walk with God.

He will not send you out until you have been tested, refined, and strengthened—ready not only for the assignment but also for the opposition. The enemy will try to distract and derail you, but God ensures that you are equipped to stand firm.

As God works on us in each season we go through, He is also working on where you're heading and the people and places you will encounter next. God is shaping all of us to fit into His plans. You may be waiting on God for an open door, while others are waiting for you to arrive on the other side.

God is present everywhere, and He is working in all these places simultaneously to prepare us, our launch, and our market to be ready for us. It's not just about you or me— it's about people, places, regions, and timing.

"Let us not grow weary in doing good, for at the proper time we will reap a harvest if we do not give up" **(Galatians 6:9).**

Just like a product that goes through design, testing, and refinement before it reaches the end user, God shapes us through every stage of the process. Timing is everything, and in His perfect timing, everything aligns exactly as it should. So, trust the process. Stay in rhythm with Him.

And when the time is right, you won't just arrive—you'll be ready. Timing is everything, and the quality of your entire process— from the sketch and notes in your journal to the end user—is connected. Seasons come and go, and the timing of the Lord is everything — not to be first or to be ahead, but to be in the sweet spot of the Kairos moment, the fullness of time.

"When the fullness of time had come, God sent forth His Son, born of a woman, born under the law, to redeem those who were under the law so that we might receive adoption as sons" **(Galatians 4:4-5).**

When it was the full divine timing, Jesus came. He was

sent in, and everything was perfectly aligned with the
divine, spiritual, historical, and prophetic timing of
the ages.

Everything was established by the hand of Yahweh, the
Alpha and Omega. It was all arranged by God, for Christ
to be revealed, from the beginning. Before anything was
created, He was there, and at the perfect time for all
creation, He entered our world and saved us. Timing is
critical in execution. There's a right time for everything—
waiting for God's timing is part of the process God takes
all His people through if they are willing.

"He changes times and seasons; he deposes kings and raises up others. He gives wisdom to the wise and knowledge to the discerning" **(Daniel 2:21).**

Finding Your Cadence and Walking in God's Rhythm

One thing you will learn—I hope—is your own personal
walk with God. A walk that is in perfect lockstep with
Him. One that is authentically yours and finds you exactly
where you're supposed to be, when you're supposed to be
there. Over the years, you'll discover your own rhythm
with God—because in the end, you're not going to be held
accountable for anyone else's walk with God, only
your own.

"Since we are living by the Spirit, let us follow the Spirit's leading in every part of our lives" **(Galatians 5:25).**

Walking in step with God means following His rhythm
and His cadence—being trained step by step to march
with Christ.

When new U.S. Army recruits go off to basic training, they're uniformed from head to toe—haircuts, pressed BDUs (Basic Dress Uniforms), and shiny boots—and given a basic training manual that they must memorize quickly. You'd better be laced up tight, boots shining, and your manual in your hands because everything you wear and do will be tested.

All of that is to get everyone on the same page—literally. To prepare soldiers to form up, stand together, and move out ready for battle. And the very first thing they teach you? How to line up in formation, and then how to march—and march a lot. And yes, how to hurry up and wait.

We were trained to fall in quickly, get into position, and then "move out" in unison. And to do it with rhythm. The drill sergeants would start singing the cadence, and we'd respond back, step by step.

Your mama was home when you LEFT... your RIGHT. Your sister was home when you LEFT... your RIGHT! Sound off! One, two. Sound off! Three, four. Sound off! One-two...three-four!

It may sound silly, but since the advent of modern armies, formation and marching have been the bedrock of military actions, and they work. One voice. One step. One direction. Squads became companies, companies became battalions, and all of us learned from the same manual, had the same haircut, and dressed exactly right. All marching to the same beat, all trained the same way.

The point? To get us in perfect rhythm. To move as one.

In the same way, walking with God means learning His rhythm. His pace. His voice. And just like those cadence calls, if you listen, you'll start to hear it: the Spirit of God calling you into step.

The Holy Spirit becomes your guide, teaching you how to move, when to wait, and how to flow in sync with Heaven. So, each step you take, take it in faith. Each day, lean in. Trust Him. And learn your own rhythm and cadence with God—the one He wrote into your spirit from the beginning.

"The Lord directs the steps of the godly. He delights in every detail of their lives" **(Psalm 37:23).**

CHAPTER 8
THE SEASONS THAT SHAPE US

"For everything there is a season, a time for every activity under heaven"
(Ecclesiastes 3:1).

Who doesn't love the change of seasons? On the East Coast, many of us love the fall for its vibrant colors and cool temperatures—the flannels and sweaters, and the start of college football.

These seasons in the natural realm of our lives vary from one region to the next, but in most of our country, we have four main ones: spring, summer, fall, and winter, and each of them comes and goes as they blend into each other.

Unless you live in Florida, Arizona, or Hawaii, you typically have two: hot and less hot. Often, these seasons are distinct, as we know, and yet some don't transition smoothly into the next. They seem to kick and scream before finally letting go of their place in the weather timetable, but eventually, they give way.

Each one has a purpose; each follows a set, designed plan to bring their time and elements to the landscape and produce what we need to eat and live. Even the sun, the moon, and the Earth's rotation have seasons and times. There are seasons in the spirit that come and go, and in each one, we are meant to learn something from the Lord for our life's lessons. As we navigate these seasons, they will produce godly fruit that remains in us.

Each season brings renewal. God is not recycling our old life — He is making us new. As one season closes, another opens, not as a repeat, but as a progression. How we exit one season prepares the soil for the next. In Christ, the old gives way to the new, and every step forward is His craftsmanship at work for us. Everything God does is redemptive; everything he does for us is to make us new.

"Therefore, if anyone is in Christ, the new creation has come: The old has gone, the new is here!" **(1 Corinthians 5:17).**

Divine Discipline Through Seasons

"Because the Lord disciplines the one He loves, and He chastens everyone He accepts as His son" **(Hebrews 12:6).**

Every season we walk through in life is a form of divine discipline—a time of training. The Greek word for discipline, "paideuō," means to train or instruct, particularly in the manner of raising a child. When God disciplines us, He is not punishing us; He is training us. He has accepted us in Christ, and now, through every season, He is shaping us into the image of His Son. Because He loves us, and we are His workmanship.

Consider the Olympic Games, specifically the gymnastics event. Each athlete competes in various disciplines—the floor exercises, the rings, the bars, and the balance beam. Every event is a unique challenge that requires skill, endurance, and perseverance. Just as gymnasts train in various disciplines to perfect their craft, we go through different seasons of training in our spiritual walk.

One season may focus on faith, another on giving, and another on waiting. Each discipline refines us, perfecting us in different ways. But no season lasts forever. They come and go by the grace of God, and we must not view the Lord's discipline as hardship to be resented, but as a gift to be embraced.

"For it is God who works in you to will and to act in order to fulfill His good purpose" **(Philippians 2:13).**

God is always working within us—daily, moment by moment, and often during seasons that stretch and shape us. What may feel like difficulty today is, in reality, preparation for what's ahead. His discipline is a mark of His love and a sign that He is actively molding us into something greater.

So, let's trust the process. Let's endure the training. Because in the end, we are not just competing for a gold medal—we are being transformed into the likeness of Christ Himself. Our focus during these changing times is on Jesus and what is happening within us, and not just what's happening to us. No matter what, we know that since we are in Christ, things don't just happen to us; they happen for us. There are seasons of separation, change, and transition.

God will dispose of things, people, and situations in our various seasons as we are pursuing Him. He will take us through a wintery pruning season, cutting away what's unnecessary and preparing us for a spring bloom in our faith. There will be times and seasons when we learn who He is through isolation and slow-down periods, where we discover He is enough for us. Only to have Him raise us in due time.

After we have gone through the testing and changing from one season to another, like spring, He renews us again. They can last from a few months to a few years. It all depends on the fruit that God is after in us to produce.

From Faith to Faith

"Those who cleanse themselves from the latter will be instruments for special purposes, made holy, useful to the Master and prepared to do any good work" **(2 Timothy 2:21).**

God is developing us from season to season and from faith to faith, preparing us for people, places, and times that God has ordained.

And it is God who is working all of this together like a great meal, like a huge holiday feast. God is at work all day in the kitchen, chopping and cutting. Prepping, salting, seasoning, and setting the table, including arranging settings and seating. The aroma of all the food is battering your nostrils and filling you with such anticipation, creating such hunger. And there is nothing you can do to help but wait until everything is ready and all the guests arrive.

It's not just a meal for you; it's a meal for everyone, and you're there as the special guest in your season. God doesn't need our help; He needs our surrender, our abiding, as He prepares the meal. He is also making a meal out of us, and in every new season, there is new wine, and new wineskins must be made.

Not only are we being prepared as a meal for the world to partake in, but we are also being remade and reshaped to hold the new anointing of the new wine of the Spirit for a new assignment, position, and place. We are the body of Christ; we are His body, and we are His meat and drink to this world. Every few years, God leads us from one season into another. And we find ourselves in the transition, asking God so many questions. But he is steady at work in the kitchen.

As God renews us by His Spirit and the washing of the Word, we are, day by day and season by season, in the Lord's hand, and He is making all things new from within us.

We shall go ... from faith to faith, and from glory to glory **(2 Timothy 2:1).**

The more we are immersed in the river of His presence, the more our brokenness is washed away. The more God stretches our faith, the greater our capacity to receive from Him. The more we pour into the Word of God, the more it pours into our spirit. All we need to do, despite any feelings of doubt, is to repeat the process in a relational way, drawing closer to God as we go.

Don't rush the process of anything you are endeavoring to create. You can't push a product to market before you have the capacity to mass-produce it with both quality and consistency. Trust me, if you rush the season or attempt to move ahead of God's timing, you will eventually have to start over. Then you will be praying, repenting, and asking God to redeem the time that was lost and heal you of the wounds you've picked up. And he will, but it's not a good time.

Seasons come and seasons go. How we leave one season is how we will enter the next, for they are sequential. We must value each season by embracing the changing times and trusting the process God is guiding us through.

"He has made everything beautiful in its time" **(Ecclesiastes 3:11).**

So, we can relax and rest in the knowledge that the times and seasons of our lives are in the hands of the Lord. He alone determines our comings and goings. Our responsibility is to follow Him as He leads and guides us by His Spirit into all truth. Every season varies in length, and with each one, God adds and removes—people, weaknesses, blind spots—and instills and works into us so much more. This is a lifelong process of growing up into the image of the Son.

CHAPTER 9
THE OPPOSITION THAT SHARPENS US

*"For a great and effective door
has opened to me, and there are many adversaries"*
(1 Corinthians 16:9).

take. Elisha then tore his own robe, symbolizing the tearing up of the old and his commitment to embrace the new, Elijah's mantle.

He then went to the Jordan and used Elijah's mantle, parting the waters just as his master and father had, stepping fully now forward into his new role and new season in life. Elisha faced 50 other prophets who were on the other side before he crossed over, and they all chose not to follow. Whether it was their lack of devotion or not being assigned to the same path, they simply did not go, and there was some opposition to the young prophet.

Yet again, not everyone can and will go into your next season or assignment; you, at times, must cross alone with whom God assigns.

"Now the sons of the prophets who were at Jericho came to Elisha and said to him, 'Do you know that the LORD will take away your master from over you today?' So Elisha answered, Yes, I know; keep silent!" **(2 Kings 2:5).**

Elisha pressed past the opposition he faced on the east side of the Jordan to the west and began the journey. This transition moment faced opposition, both from Elijah in his testing of his young protégé and from the other prophets. But he and Elisha walked through it. Opposition often comes before or alongside the opening of a door, signaling that a transition is happening. We need to keep that opposition on the outside of us and not allow it to be internalized and walk through the door God opens.
In all things we walk by faith and not by sight, we give God our yes, and we follow.

CHAPTER 10
BE STILL

"Be still and know that I am God"
(Psalm 46:10).

Paul was presented with an open door—a clear opportunity to advance the gospel—and yet, in his own words, that door came with opposition. He writes to the Corinthian church, expressing his deep desire to be with them, but decides to stay in Ephesus for a little longer because of the great and effective work that is happening there. This is a powerful reminder that opposition often accompanies opportunity.

Just because a door is open does not mean the path will be easy. In fact, resistance is often a sign that the opportunity is significant. Paul did not shrink back when challenges arose; instead, he recognized that God was moving powerfully and that the opposition was simply part of the process. It appears that Paul had other ministry happening on the side, and as this new door opened, he was excited but also aware of the struggles that came with it.

Yet, he was not discouraged. He understood that opposition is often the final barrier before stepping into a new season. This pattern is also true in our own lives. Before we transition into a new opportunity, we may face resistance—spiritual, emotional, or even circumstantial. The enemy does not fight what is stagnant; he fights what is advancing. But just as Paul stood firm, so must we.

Opposition is not a stop sign—it is often a confirmation that you are on the right path. We see this pattern throughout Scripture: Nehemiah faced opposition when rebuilding the walls of Jerusalem, but he pressed on, knowing that God had called him to the work. Jesus Himself experienced intense opposition just before stepping into His greatest work—His death and resurrection. The Israelites faced opposition the very night prior to crossing the Red Sea, just before stepping into their deliverance.

Today, we and the world are in a transitional moment where the old will give way to the new—in the kingdom, the church, the nation, and within individuals. Just as Moses made way for Joshua, transitions in leadership are happening now. When there is a transition from one season to the next, or from one generation to the next, there is often opposition we must walk through.

Transitions

Elisha and Joshua both left one season, submitted to their parents, spiritual fathers, and leaders to become the ones to carry the weight of their own callings. They left one season and entered the next season. Their transitions were marked by challenges. This is because you cannot lead if you have not followed. You cannot give what you do not have.

You cannot give wise, sage advice to the next generation unless you have learned it in your own time, under circumstances God ordained and to which you submitted. Jesus learned obedience through what He suffered, and He also learned to follow—in private—before promotion came. We cannot skip steps. We cannot cheat or cut corners, regardless of who is watching or not. Private experiences develop and test character, which is then revealed publicly. Character matters a lot—it is the red carpet for the anointing of your life. If that carpet stops and the anointing continues, it will only be a matter of time before you run out of both.

the Baptist was beheaded, Paul almost had a fist fight with Barnabas, and even Moses had to give way to Joshua and Caleb.

Transitions are not all the same, but they happen, and we will experience many of them as we grow and advance in this kingdom. God always wants us to be fresh, ready, and prepared; the old must go before the new arrives. Opposition is often an indicator that a door is opening.

"Behold, I will send you Elijah the prophet before the coming of the great and dreadful day of the Lord. He will turn the hearts of fathers to their children, and the hearts of children to their fathers, or I will curse the earth" **(Malachi 4:5-6).**

Elisha was marked by Elijah early on as someone anointed by the Lord, and he kept his eye on him. Elijah crossed the Jordan and parted it with his mantle, and Elisha followed, even though Elijah tried to discourage him by telling him not to follow.

Elisha was devoted, determined, and disciplined; he pursued. Like a fresh baptism, or a crossing from the old into the new, Elijah parted the waters as Elisha followed closely behind—much like Joshua pursued Moses up Mount Sinai. Elisha pressed past the test and obstacle.

Again, testing the young prophet—his master and father—stopped and asked Elisha, "What do you want me to do for you?" And Elisha replied, "I want a double portion of your anointing." "If you see me when I am taken up from you, it shall be so," he replied. Elisha continued to follow his spiritual father until he saw God take him up to heaven in a fiery chariot. His mantle dropped for Elisha to

We need to persevere while serving in inferior positions and under leaders whom God places us under, who may not have our best interests at heart. We may have a greater calling or a larger group to lead one day, but we will never advance in God's kingdom authority by cutting corners or having a critical attitude. The greater the weight of the calling, the greater the testing you will experience.

Transitions are not easy; they are not clean-cut. It's all different, but the principles remain the same—we have to leave something, or sometimes everything, before we can receive the new. Israel crossed over with death on their heels, Abraham leaving his nephew Lot behind, Jesus being taken up, and all His followers watching Him ascend, just as Elijah did before Elisha. Transitions cost us something, and opposition and revelation usually arrive just before the door opens.

Jesus said, "And no one puts new wine into old wineskins; or else the new wine will burst the wineskins and be spilled, and the wineskins will be ruined. But new wine must be put into new wineskins, and both are preserved" **(Luke 5:37-38)**.

Not everyone can go with us into the next season—not everyone and not everything. Old friends, old habits, and even old wine. The way you did things in the last few years may not be the way the Lord wants to do them in the next few years in your life and ministry. A separation may come, and it may be significant. Every season before this one has been preparing you to become a new wineskin.

With that came times of isolation and separation, the ending of relationships—sometimes for a season, sometimes forever. Elijah was caught up to heaven, John

The primary purpose of waiting and being still before the Lord is to allow God to take us into His hands and begin to work in us only that which His divine nature can. Waiting is where we stop, and God begins.

Waiting is like the bonding or binding agent in cooking or science—it is what makes everything come together: God's timing and your footsteps. In everyday life and in the waiting seasons and times, to be still is an inward thing as much as an outward one. To be still, as in stop striving, and trying to do this in your own strength and ways.

Be still and *"Know that I am God,"* that I am *"Good."* Waiting, in essence, is where we stop, and God begins, where God can do his deepest work in our inner man. The Hebrew word for "wait" is **"Qavah"** which means to wait actively with anticipation, hopefully watching for God to act. Looking to the horizon for His promises to come. It literally means to be tent-pegged to the ground, roped in, and intertwined with the Lord.

We are waiting with God and for God. So, it is much better to be strapped in with God, rested, and ready at the same time. This isn't passive sitting around—this is an active expectation. This is positioning yourself like a watchman on the wall, scanning the horizon for the breakthrough you know is coming. This is being so connected to God that you move when He moves, rest when He rests, and rise when He says "Now."

"But those who hope in the LORD will renew their strength. They will soar on wings like eagles; they will run and not grow weary, they will walk and not be faint" **(Isaiah 40:31).**

Fruit That Feeds the World

The waiting and testing produce lasting fruit in us—fruit that will nourish the world. We are not just bearing fruit; we are becoming the fruit that others will partake of. The results of waiting vary from season to season, yet it is always to bring forth something new from within us. Something born from discipline. To learn obedience or to learn patience. Times of learning to trust God for all your needs and times of reflection and preparation.

"A good man brings good things out of the good stored up in him" **(Matthew 12:35).**

We cannot give away what we do not have. And God wants to give us all things. It isn't just material; it is ethereal, it is spirit, and it is maturity. And waiting is a method God uses to shape us into His image. God always maximizes the waiting period. He is continually working for our good, and we must be diligent in our days to prepare for both present and future seasons of action.

"And we know that in all things God works for the good of those who love him, who have been called according to his purpose" **(Romans 8:28).**

The Enemy's Attack During Waiting

"Be very careful, then, how you live—not as unwise but as wise, making the most of every opportunity, because the days are evil" **(Ephesians 5:15-16).**

In these seasons of waiting and preparation, we trust that He who began a good work in us will complete it. The enemy will attempt to sow discord, division, and confusion, but we must remain vigilant. He will come and try to get you to move off your spot before it's time. To be impulsive and to run ahead. He will use your own inside voice to make you move before your time.

The harvest is coming; the night cannot last forever. Our goal is to abide in Him with an inner peace, laboring to be still and resisting the temptation to lean on our own strength and understanding.

To abide and trust is another form of worship. It declares to the world and to the enemy where our true trust lies. God is working in us right now, preparing us, and the key to waiting well is to let God do His work completely.

Secret Encounters in the Waiting

Waiting and trusting teach us how to hear His voice and to learn how to follow His inward witness to us. For example, at three in the morning, prompting you to get up and get your Bible, even when you're so tired. You have been thinking about God all day and need His love.

Yet you struggle to obey and get up because it doesn't make sense. Yet you do with faith, then you find Jesus waiting in your favorite place, inviting you to come and sit in an encounter with Him.

You're blown away by his simplicity, his affection, and his pursuit of your heart. You're stunned and filled with awe, and again he marks your heart, and you just fall deeper in love with him. These moments come only to the very few who will rise and go to the unusual places, at unusual times, in out-of-the-ordinary moments, to meet with Him apart from the crowds.

We get these moments with God because we have positioned ourselves before God in prayer and in our hearts. He always wants to draw you into the deep places of His heart to show us how deeply He cares for us.

As the Bible says, "He made known his ways to Moses, his deeds to the people of Israel" **(Psalm 103:7).**

Israel knew God's acts, but Moses knew God's ways. And for us today, we can know God's ways—His desires, His thoughts. We can know God. We can know His mind, and all this comes from waiting upon the Lord and dwelling with Him.

The Mocking Voices

"Now the serpent was more crafty than any of the wild animals the LORD God had made. He said to the woman, 'Did God really say, "You must not eat from any tree in the garden"? **(Genesis 3:1).**

"Did God say" is the voice of the accuser of the brethren, and the source of active measures and subversive actions meant to make us beat ourselves by causing us to question who we are and what we are and accusing God to us. When we are waiting, we are in a vulnerable state—a place between the promise and the promised land, where the enemy will come to sow seeds of doubt, confusion, and discord in our minds.

His goal is to unsettle us and try to get us to move from our position of faith into action too soon. The Devil is always lurking and looking for ways to cause us to expose ourselves to unnecessary attacks from our enemy. Yet this is where we need to hold firm in our current position, rest, wait, and trust in God's nature to keep His "bond" with us.

The phrase "Did God say?" is intended to cast doubt within us and prompt us to question God, thereby attempting to sow division and confusion in our minds. Lucifer is the god of the airwaves, the god of propaganda and lies, and even the very father of lies. His nature is rebellious and subversive, and he relishes his role of chief saboteur of the children of God.

Standing Firm in the Wait

"Therefore put on the full armor of God, so that when the day of evil comes, you may be able to stand your ground, and after you have done everything, to stand" **(Ephesians 6:13).**

While we wait in God's waiting rooms, while we are in the most vulnerable state in waiting and quiet, the voice of the mocker often comes. And it can even come from our friends and families—often in seemingly well-meaning ways—but always meant to discourage, distract, and disillusion us, as seen in the case of Job.

That voice of the accuser, which comes to get us to overthink and doubt, comes to test and tempt us. "Did God really say, ' Sit and wait? The voices come, trying to cause us to be double-minded and confused.

It involves accusing God of abandoning us or accusing us of being disobedient and full of faults, which shifts our focus from God to ourselves. All of this comes to sow doubt in what we know and have heard, trying to get us to abandon our position and step away from the place where God has placed us. The Mocker's voice comes from the accuser, the devil, and it can sound very much like our own voice. It tries to lead us away from the path of the promise God has made for us.

Abraham had the promise given, the provision, and the experience, and yet failed to wait through to the promise, creating problems for all of us.

From Abiding to Victory

"Abide in Me, and I in you....and you will bear much fruit" **(John 15).**

As we wait, we must learn to lean into and abide in the vine of Christ, trusting His lordship over our lives. He will turn the temptation into a test that will only make us stronger in our weakest places. The battle then transfers from the realm of victory in the spirit to a struggle in the mud of our minds; we can then go from abiding to striving.

If you find yourself in this moment, understand that both God and the devil are after something in you—one to deceive you into giving up or moving too soon, the devil, that is. The other seeks to use this moment to shape and transform us into the very image of His Son—that is, our Abba.

The battle is already won, if God has already spoken or shown us the path. All we need to do is do the next right thing and focus on the day we are in, with no worried thoughts about tomorrow. The enemy wants us to give up on ourselves before we even get started, or to stop trusting

God, or to give in and run ahead of God. This often leads us into all sorts of entanglements by trying to fulfill a legitimate need in an illegitimate way.

Waiting is where we end and God begins, and the Mocker's Voice, that subversive voice, will come and try to tempt you by saying, "Did God say?"

The goal is to remain patient and abide in God's timing, trusting in His character and nature, while ignoring the lies and taking captive the mocker's voice. Get it settled in your heart, and you will rise with eagles' wings.

CHAPTER 11
THE BATTLE FOR HEARTS AND MINDS

*"Do not conform to the pattern of this world,
but be transformed by the renewing of your mind.
Then you will be able to test and approve
what God's will is—his good, pleasing and perfect will"*
(Romans 12:2).

The Voice of God brings peace and encouragement, yet the voice of the accuser brings judgment and condemnation. The Victory is won, but the battle now is in the mind, and we wage war with God's word for the washing and the renewing of our minds.

The battle is for the hearts and minds of all humanity, and who we will believe, follow, and worship.

The god of this age has blinded the minds of unbelievers, so that they cannot see the light of the gospel that displays the glory of Christ, who is the image of God" **(2 Corinthians 4:4).**

Lucifer is a narcissistic, gaslighting fallen angel and the prince and power of the air—so he is also the prince and power of the airwaves and transmissions. He is the source of all propaganda, lies, and accusations. He controls the narrative through all major mainstream media outlets.

He manipulates the truth, bending it, recasting it, and gaslighting us. He is the source of all accusations that we see in the media and politics. His goal is to accuse God, to throw shame on God's name, and to defame His image in our hearts and minds.

"When he lies, he speaks his native language, for he is a liar and the father of lies" **(John 8:44).**

Satan will come during your weak moments or when you make a huge mistake, and he will take that open window and say, "Look at you, look at what you did, that's who you are." If you agree, you will be led down a rabbit hole of thoughts that will depress you and lead to self-hatred and judgment.

But Jesus never does that. Jesus says, "Look at me." And when you look at Him, you remember who He is and remember who you are, and you repent of what you did.

The devil says, "Look at what you did," while Jesus says, "Look at me." You see, it is his kindness that leads you to repentance. The sin is dealt with. It's under the blood. It's over.

"So now there is no condemnation for those who belong to Christ Jesus" **(Romans 8:1).**

One day, I was in the middle of one of the toughest battles of my life. Spiritual warfare was fierce. Anxiety and confusion swirled all around me. I had malaria. I was trapped inside my head. I was in a war. The enemy whispered lies. Condemnation tried to take hold in my soul. I felt weak, tired, and vulnerable. Then, in the stillness of my tent, Jesus came. He spoke to me—not in a thunderclap, but in clarity: "Rick," He said, "I never condemn."

It hit me like lightning. I answered, "Yes, Lord." But again, he said it—stronger this time. "I never condemn ever."

At that moment, I knew Jesus had just stepped into my tent. There was no guilt in His voice. No pressure. No shame. Just the truth. Love. Peace. Shalom. His wisdom was present. His voice was full of mercy. His glory had filled that little tent in Zambia with the very nature of God.

His goodness, his mercy, his long-suffering, and his kindness were all there with me, leaning in as he spoke to me, so that not a word of condemnation would appear from his mouth.

The Prince of Propaganda

He can't bring God down, but he works to bring God down in the minds and eyes of humanity. He wants to fill our minds, then our hearts, with such deception and shame that we will give up and walk away from God. He wants to use our own headspace against us by infiltrating it with his twisted views and causing us to come into agreement with his lies.

"For our struggle is not against flesh and blood, but against the rulers, against the authorities, against the powers of this dark world and against the spiritual forces of evil in the heavenly realms" **(Ephesians 6:12).**

Spiritual warfare is asymmetrical warfare: when something is asymmetrical, it means it's uneven, unbalanced, or not the same on both sides. It doesn't follow a mirrored or matching pattern. Asymmetrical warfare is the devil's bread and butter. Nothing he does is measured or aligned; his attacks will come at you from anywhere, at any time, and from anyone.

He doesn't need to destroy us head-on. He just needs to divide us, distract us, and make us distrust each other long enough to burn the house down from the inside.

Using Us Against Ourselves

Twisting our beliefs, using unresolved issues within us that open doors to demonic outside pressures. Satan can weaken us from the inside with his spiritual knowledge concerning our lives; he uses us against ourselves, and it costs him nothing.

"But each person is tempted when they are dragged away by their own evil desire and enticed" **(James 1:14).**

Temptation is our own inward evil desires, the Bible says, and that is what Satan uses against us and tempts us with what we already want.

"Yet we submit to God and thus resist the devil and he will flee " **(James 4:7).**

We all must clear out all unresolved issues in our hearts as God reveals them to us. These are open doors to our mind, will, and emotions. This is what nations do to other nations during conflict: they identify the weak spots, the dirt, the secrets, and use them to gain leverage for manipulation.

Satan is unmeasured, narcissistic, and determined to fill what God loves most—us—with what he hates most—him. Satan, using our own voice in our heads, plans to penetrate deeply into our wills—this is subversion; it is asymmetrical spiritual warfare.

YET!

Taking Every Thought Captive

"We demolish arguments and every pretension that sets itself up against the knowledge of God, and we take captive every thought to make it obedient to Christ" **(2 Corinthians 10:5).**

We must know the Word of God and understand what God says, so we can take all these intrusive, lying thoughts captive and replace them with the truth of God's Word.

We must replace the lies with the truths of Scripture, and we have that authority. Jesus said, "All authority in heaven and earth has been given to me, so ask whatever you like in my name, and I will do it."

"Very truly I tell you, whoever believes in me will do the works I have been doing, and they will do even greater things than these, because I am going to the Father. And I will do whatever you ask in my name, so that the Father may be glorified in the Son" **(John 14:12-13).**

Begin by identifying the lies and writing them down. Then, look up the scriptures to combat those lies and arrest them—take them captive and replace them with what Jesus says.

"No weapon forged against you will prevail, and you will refute every tongue that accuses you. This is the heritage of the servants of the LORD, and this is their vindication from me," declares the LORD **(Isaiah 54:17).**

The Battle for Your Headspace

We must take control of our headspace because it controls what we think, what we believe about ourselves, about God, and about others. We cannot continue to surrender any longer to the prince of the air and allow him to defeat us by getting us to self-destruct. The enemy's strategy is simple: if he can control the narrative in your mind, he can control your actions.

If he can get you to believe his lies about your identity, your worth, your calling, your God—then he's won without firing a shot. But here's what he doesn't want you to know: you have authority over your own thought life. You don't have to accept every thought that pops into your head. You don't have to agree with every accusation, every doubt, every fear that tries to set up camp in your mind.

Your Authority in Christ

"Behold, I have given you authority to tread on serpents and scorpions, and over all the power of the enemy, and nothing shall hurt you" **(Luke 10:19).**

When you got saved, you didn't just get forgiveness—you got authority. You didn't just get a ticket to heaven—you got weapons for the war. You didn't just get a new identity—you got the power to defend it.

"When you believed, you were marked in him with a seal, the promised Holy Spirit" **(Ephesians 1:13).**

You are marked by God and sealed with the Holy Spirit. The enemy knows this, and that's why he's working so hard to make you forget it. That's why the battle is so intense for your mind—because he knows if he loses there, he's lost you completely. But you're not fighting this battle in your own strength.

You're not relying on your own willpower or positive thinking. You are wielding the sword of the Spirit, which is the Word of God. You're standing on promises that cannot be broken.

The Victory is Already Won

"But thanks be to God who gives us the victory through our Lord Jesus Christ" **(1 Corinthians 15:57).**

In the kingdom where we live, the victory is already won for us. We go from victory—the cross—to victory—heaven—and He has provided everything we need. He has given you the armor and weapons, along with real-time power through the Holy Spirit. He has given you a manual—the Word of God—and instant communication through the inward witness of His Spirit and full support for this new life or campaign you're on. He has even personally defeated the enemy.

"It is finished" **(John 19:30).**

It is finished and has given you all the authority you will need to move through this world.

The battle for your heart and mind is real, but the outcome is not in question. You are more than a conqueror through Him who loved you. Now it's time to start acting like it.

Get Off the X

"For God has not given us a spirit of fear, but of power and of love and of a sound mind" **(2 Timothy 1:7).**

In World War II, the German army had decimated almost all of Europe and was advancing unhindered towards England, and the world was at war. When the United States entered the fight, we decided to invade Europe from multiple locations, but the biggest one was from the beaches of France, known as Normandy and Omaha.

The entire U.S. Navy had amassed in the Atlantic Ocean, bombing the German army that was entrenched along the French coast above the sandy beaches. They had massive bunkers and forts along the beach, high up on the sand dunes, with all of France captured behind them.

The U.S. Military began launching smaller boats carrying soldiers onto the beaches. The average age of those "men" was around 21 years, as they faced relentless machine guns and bombs coming at them from the German batteries, and we lost thousands of our ancestors.

The Only Way to Survive

As the "men"—those still alive—landed on the beach or water, their first command was to get off the beach and hide under the machine guns of the Germans beneath the sand dunes. They were being shot to pieces, and many men, out of fear, hesitated, trying to find cover and lie down. But they simply were shot to pieces. All those who understood were yelling and running forward:

"GET OFF THE BEACH! GET OFF THE BEACH!"

As long as they remained stagnant and tried to hide, they were easy targets, and they would die. The only safety was under the guns of the Germans, so the command and the lifeline were to get off the beach. But many, understandably, were gripped by fear, and they succumbed to it and didn't make it off the beach—heroes one and all, yet they are not here with us.

The only way to survive a real-world enemy ambush is to GET OFF THE X. As quickly as possible, you must recognize the ambush, fight back, and get off the X and out of the kill zone. You Joined the Army.

"When you believed, you were marked in him with a seal, the promised Holy Spirit" **(Ephesians 1:13).**

The moment you got saved, you joined an army—the army of God—and then immediately you became a target of Satan and anyone who aligns with him in humanity. You became a light to the world and a light in the darkness. You are now marked by God and sealed with the Holy Spirit, and now you have become the enemy of our enemy.

You are now on the X or the spot where the warfare is strongest, and Satan has ordered you to be shot by a demonic machine gun in your thoughts. You must learn to defend yourself with God's word, understand your position and authority, and always move forward under His wings.

Don't Stay Static

But you have the power to get off the beach, to get off the X and move forward under the protection of God's covering, and to move forward deeper and deeper into Christ, and to live a very dynamic life with God—and that is how to win.

Yes, there will be attacks over time, but we have already been given the victory in Christ. In fact, we live from victory to victory. We have been seated with Christ in heavenly places, and we are hidden by God in Christ.

Yet we still cannot remain stagnant—we must continue to move forward in our walk with Christ. You will survive and thrive if you push forward and deeper and deeper into God's protection, under His wings, to be hidden by God in Christ.

"He will cover you with his feathers, and under his wings you will find refuge; his faithfulness will be your shield and rampart" **(Psalm 91:4).**

Take the Fight to the Enemy

We cannot quit, we cannot stop, and we cannot give one inch to Satan in our minds. We must rise from where we are and move forward in prayer and the Word. We must begin to pray and worship, change the atmosphere, and move off the beach. Past the bullets and the bombs of the enemy, deflecting them with the shield of faith and the helmet of salvation, and go into attack mode up the dunes into the enemy's camp and take back what was lost.

"In addition to all this, take up the shield of faith, with which you can extinguish all the flaming arrows of the evil one. Take the helmet of salvation and the sword of the Spirit, which is the word of God" **(Ephesians 6:16-17).**

"But thanks be to God who gives us the victory through our Lord Jesus Christ. Therefore, my beloved brothers, be firm, steadfast, always fully devoted to the work of the Lord, knowing that in the Lord your labor is not in vain" **(1 Corinthians 15:57-58).**

He has given you a manual—the Word of God—and

instant communication through the inward witness of His Spirit and full support for this new life or campaign you're on. He has even personally defeated the enemy already—

"It is finished" **(John 19:30).**

It is finished and has given you all the authority you will need to move through this world. Yet there is spiritual warfare, and it is a real battle every day; we just need to focus on the victory provided and assert our authority and dominance through our positions in Christ.

For Such a Time as This

"And who knows but that you have come to your royal position for such a time as this?" **(Esther 4:14).**

You didn't get saved by accident. You weren't born into this generation by chance. You weren't given your specific gifts, your unique background, your particular experiences randomly.

The enemy knows this, which is why he's working so hard to keep you pinned down on the beach. He knows what you're capable of when you get off the X and start moving in the authority Christ has given you.

He knows the damage you can do to his kingdom when you stop playing defense and go on the offensive. But here's what he doesn't want you to know: his attacks are confirmation that you're a threat.

The enemy doesn't waste ammunition on people who aren't a danger to his plans. If you're under heavy fire, it's because you matter. It's because your breakthrough will impact not just you, but everyone around you.

The Command is Clear

So, what's your response going to be? Are you going to stay pinned down on the beach, taking hit after hit, hoping somehow the enemy will get tired and leave you alone? Or are you going to remember who you are, who you are, and what authority you carry?

The command is clear: GET OFF THE X.

Stop being a sitting duck for the enemy's lies. Stop giving him free real estate in your mind. Stop accepting defeat as a normal part of Christian life. Get up! Move forward. Take the fight to the enemy.

Your breakthrough is on the other side of your breakthrough mindset. Your victory is on the other side of your willingness to engage. Your destiny is on the other side of your decision to stop surviving and start thriving. The beach is no place for a child of the King. It's time to storm the enemy's strongholds and take back what he's stolen.

"From the days of John the Baptist until now, the kingdom of heaven has been subjected to violence, and violent people have been raiding it" **(Matthew 11:12).**

Let's take back what's ours!

CHAPTER 12
THE VOLUNTEERS:
EMBRACE THE PROCESS

"And who knows but that you have come to your royal position for such a time as this?"
(Esther 4:14).

You have come into the kingdom, and now you have tasted the goodness of Jesus, and you're like, I want more, I need more of you, God.

And so, you asked God to separate you from the ordinary and the normal. You asked Him to remove anything in your heart that isn't pleasing to Him, and you asked God for the fire of testing to come upon your heart, and you began to raise your hand and move forward to the altar every day in your heart.

Then God said, "Sure thing, let's move into a higher form of walking with me." You are now hungering even more for His word and for His presence, and nothing else satisfies. It is now a moment of consecration and to sell out all the way.

From Infantry to Special Forces.

I love the comparison between the military and the kingdom of heaven because they align so well that it is easy to draw parallels. Let's look at the U.S. Army Infantry in comparison to the Kingdom of Heaven and the Church. Here begins your faith journey and service as an infantryman or spiritual foot soldier, like the US Army's 11B (Bravo), and now you're part of the Church Army.

You fully enlisted and were trained in all the basics of spiritual life and warfare. You spiritually grow up in the local church under the guidance of amazing leaders and elders. Then, maybe you start sensing God's calling to join in the outreaches and missions of your church, but now you want more.

You want to take the road less traveled, where it begins to narrow, and you start hungering for the deeper life of a soldier for Christ—to go from holding the spear to becoming a part of the spear, and maybe one day the tip of it.

Now, you want to transition from the regular church army infantry to the volunteer unit. I don't mean "volunteer" in the sense of doing charity work. But you begin to raise your hand before God, asking for complex missions.

In the US Army, these are all "volunteer" regiments, and you have, in a sense, "raised your hand" and stepped out. And if your command allows, you will attempt to leave the regular Army and try for the next tier up. Maybe the Rangers, the Green Berets, or perhaps the other upper tiers of the U.S. Army. Maybe even further down the spear, to the very tip—to try out for a "special missions' unit."

Yet in the US Army, you have to volunteer even to be considered for their special mission units. You have to request to be sent to a "selection." No one can force you.

They aren't easy to even get close to. You have to be allowed to try, and then you have to qualify or make/pass a "selection." These are the Army's elite. Their attrition rates are the highest. It's rough. It's hard-nosed. That's the clearest way I can put it.

Yet those who try out are drawn by the challenge and the call to serve in the deepest capacity the Infantry has to offer.

Those who go on this path have all my love and respect because they heard something within themselves. A call to go deeper, and they step forward into the deep end.

The Macedonian Call

"During the night Paul had a vision of a man of Macedonia standing and begging him, 'Come over to Macedonia and help us'" **(Acts 16:9).**

You'll go through all sorts of selections and courses and schools, where you learn the way of the warrior and leadership that the U.S. Army has established. Each school, each squad, exists for different reasons—but with one main mission: protect Americans and free the oppressed.

And it all starts the moment you raise your hand and say, "I want more." "I want to be an Airborne Ranger." "I want to be a Green Beret." That's the beginning of your volunteering—for the sharp end.

Each time you raise your hand for MORE and each time you pass through selections/testing, the room and the people in it get smaller and smaller. As you progress down that path, you will make greater and deeper friends, but you will be in a very small community.

But it also comes with so much more freedom from the standard, regular army infantry.

You begin to go on missions and assignments in very small teams to assert your dominance over the enemies of freedom.

You begin to live in a small section of men and women who heard a call and went forward, no matter the cost.

You will dress differently, look differently, and move and serve much differently than you once did. But first you have to volunteer and be allowed, and then comesthe testing.

The same is true with God, your local church, your family, and friends: as you feel God drawing you out, you'll leave behind much of who you were. This allows you to become
all God has truly called you to be and to go where many dare not. All because you heard a call, and you answered and entered a wilderness of testing that is designed to train you and prepare you.

To teach and protect you so you can teach and protect others but first the testing.

Consecration, Testing, and Selections

As you go further and further down the road less traveled in both special missions and in the Kingdom, into selections and wilderness testing. Everything in you will hurt. Everything you thought you knew will be tested. Everything about you will be on the line, and you will be challenged to the very core, even your identity and physicality, as you progress. It will be hard, and when you feel like whining, quitting, and blaming someone, you'll have to remind yourself of one thing: no one forced you.

You volunteered.

Remember, you raised your hand to God, and you came forward as the Holy Spirit was recruiting you. And now God is honing you and reshaping you and preparing you as a spiritual weapon. And if you make it, you will join some of the most elite, self-motivated, battle-proven warriors in the world. You'll go from honorable to most honored—all because you saw something in God's presence or in his missionaries or in his word and then something in yourself.

And you said, "I want to do that." And off you went.

That's the same path many people walk in all kinds of callings—doctors, lawyers, engineers, chefs, builders, leaders. You saw something—a building being made, a meal being created, a courtroom drama, a missionary spoke at your church. And God anointed it before your eyes and in your spirit, and it lit a fire in you. And you wanted the challenge and the career, and you wanted to grow. You wanted to be more than just regular. So, you reached out to grab it. And now—you're paying the price.

You're battling through doubt, depression, anxiety, pain, and loneliness. You didn't know the cost. You didn't know what it would take. Now you're in the thick of it. It's kicking your old, lazy self down as God is raising a new you. Whether it's education, construction, medicine, law, politics, or simply breaking free from whatever holds you back, it takes inner fortitude. Strength. A resolve that says, "I will finish. I will not ring that bell. I will not quit. If I die or fail, it won't be because I gave up.

They'll have to pass me or bury me."

This is called "Grit" and perseverance, and in many cases, just stubbornness. But this is for those who don't want to sit in the pews at church, who, when they hear the stories of missionaries or the call of the needy, can't sleep; they want to help, they want to go.

Welcome to the Deeper Jesus Life

"I press on toward the goal to win the prize for which God has called me heavenward in Christ Jesus" **(Philippians 3:14).**

Welcome to the deeper Jesus life that you volunteered for, as everything I just described in the natural world is what is happening to you in the spirit. You saw something in someone else's walk with God, and it lit a fire in you. And off to the altar of consecration you went, screaming out to God. "I want more of you, I want all you have, I will go anywhere and do anything you need. Please God, pick the darkest and hardest road, and please send me."

"Then I heard the voice of the Lord saying, 'Whom shall I send? And who will go for us?' And I said, 'Here am I. Send me! **(Isaiah 6:8).**

When you said at that altar, "God, I want more," or "Use me any way You want," "Send me"—that was you volunteering for the sharp edge of God's sword. That was you burning with passion and fire, burning your ships at the beach and saying, "No turning back." That was you. Remember? That was me. That was us.

"No one who puts a hand to the plow and looks back is fit for service in the kingdom of God" **(Luke 9:62).**

You Volunteered

Now, when the road has narrowed and many of your old friends have fallen away, and your life feels like it's being radically overhauled, and you're not seeing anything but the fire...It was like John Knox in the 1500's Scotland, who was so burning for God and his own people, he cried famously to God: **"Give me Scotland, or I die."**

When God lights a fire in you… man, it burns continually until you embrace the embers and run forward, jumping headfirst into the mystery that is the call. You chose this path all on your own, albeit with a little supernatural nudge from your best friend, the Holy Spirit. It was God placing a demand on the anointing He put in you to come and answer the call to go deeper with Him and further with Him. To see nations shaken by the power of prayer and by the power of God.

You are one who can't settle for the regular army of the church, and you wanted to serve anywhere, at any time, and you cried out day and night for more of God, more, please, more. I remember for me this has been several moments from 1993 to today, as I slip in and out of various roles for the Lord, he always draws me into another moment of fiery consecration and a further stepping forward.

I remember one major day - there were many and still are - in 1994 when, at a Rodney Howard-Browne meeting in Washington, DC, the fire of God came over us, and my heart was exploding. I was burning under the fire of God's presence inside my spirit and on my physical body.

And I just wept aloud.

"Lord, I prayed, come take me and send me anywhere, I cried out in that revival meeting, Lord, please just take me anywhere that is the darkest, the most hurting, the worst place, and please use me, God...I cried out..." Blindfold me and drop me off anywhere. That moment of fiery encounters has followed me all my life, and they come at the most awkward times and unexpected moments. I know God set me up, and he gave me those desires to "Volunteer" for the deep end of the Army of God. I wanted covert operations of God.

"...when he comes, he will baptize you with the Holy Spirit and Fire" **(Matthew 3:11).**

Jesus baptizes us with the Holy Spirit and Fire!

And that Fire is our friend, and the safest place you can ever be is in the fire of God. When it comes, don't run from it; collapse and surrender under it. Fire prepares us for the Glory. You will cry out for souls and for nations and for the secret place of God. You will scream and groan and surrender and run and yell and cry, and it will burn the nonsense out of your religion. It will expose your deepest desires, and you will cry out for them. I desired deeply to travel the road and give my guts for Jesus. No matter where God needed or wanted me, I wanted it.

"When the Spirit of truth comes, he will guide you into all the truth, for he will not speak on his own authority, but whatever he hears he will speak, and he will declare to you the things that are to come" **(John 16:13).**

When Jesus, the recruiter, came to your church that one Sunday and set out an appeal for more troops or more friends to come and follow him, it was the Holy Spirit in you nudging you, saying, "Hey, let's sign up together!!!" But you're not alone. God is walking with you—step by step, from faith to faith and glory to glory.

God is the one empowering every move you make. Sanctifying you and preparing you for what you asked for and what He always wanted. He gave you the desires, and you grabbed hold of them, inspired by the Holy Spirit, and now you're running with it all. You're running with the very fire He is testing you with.

You said, "Here am I, God..." And He said, "Okay, My love. Let's go forward together." And He began theprocess of the deeper work in you as He prepares the people and the place you will go into to serve and to reveal His love and power to. He has called you into the darkness, and He has lit you on fire to bring the light of Christ.

Your True Identity

"For we are God's handiwork, created in Christ Jesus to do good works, which God prepared in advance for us to do" **(Ephesians 2:10).**

You are the light of the world. You are His son and His daughter. You are His weapon of choice, and you are becoming more and more like Him and His Son every day. You are the spitting image of your heavenly Father, created to do good works and to spread His love and image all around, and He is so proud of you.

"You are the light of the world. A town built on a hill cannot be hidden. Neither do people light a lamp and put it under a bowl.

Instead they put it on its stand, and it gives light to everyone in the house. In the same way, let your light shine before others, that they may see your good deeds and glorify your Father in heaven" **(Matthew 5:14-16).**

The room is getting smaller, but the mission is getting bigger. The path is getting narrower, but the calling is getting clearer. You volunteered for this, and God is equipping you for everything He's calling you to. Now it's time to step into the fullness of who you were created to be.

Your moment is here. Your God is proud. Let's burn for Jesus. The nations are waiting.

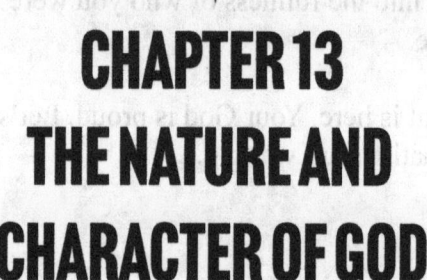

CHAPTER 13
THE NATURE AND
CHARACTER OF GOD

*"But the fruit of the Spirit is love, joy, peace, forbearance, kindness, goodness, faithfulness, gentleness and self-control.
Against such things there is no law"*
(Galatians 5:22-23).

There are two kingdoms constantly at work in this world. Just like there were two trees in the Garden of Eden, there are two forces—two spiritual realms—each marked by presence, power, and wisdom. And each one carries the nature and character of its ruler.

One is the Kingdom of Heaven, ruled by the Lord of all Glory—Jesus Christ. His Kingdom is filled with His presence, His Word, His voice, His power, and His glory. Everything within His Kingdom reflects His nature. And His nature is beautifully expressed in the fruit of the Spirit.

This divine nature fills heaven. It is in His voice, His Word, and every command He gives. When we are born again, we are transferred from the kingdom of darkness to the Kingdom of Light, and we are filled with his divine, eternal nature and presence. We are filled with his light and love.

"For he has rescued us from the dominion of darkness and brought us into the kingdom of the Son he loves, in whom we have redemption, the forgiveness of sins" **(Colossians 1:13-14).**

With this transfer, we receive a new heart and a new nature—the very nature of Jesus. We no longer walk by the carnal nature described in Galatians 5:19-21, but by the spiritual nature. As we yield to the Spirit, we begin to live from this new identity, governed by God's nature.

Worship as Warfare

"And we all, who with unveiled faces contemplate the Lord's glory, are being transformed into his image with ever-increasing glory, which comes from the Lord, who is the Spirit" **(2 Corinthians 3:18).**

Worship plays a central role in this transformation, because we become what we behold. This is why the battle for worship is so intense. Satan knows that if we behold Jesus, we will reflect His glory. We will be transformed into the image of the One we gaze upon:

But the enemy also has a kingdom. He is a fallen archangel, once perfect in beauty and wisdom, created to reflect God's glory. He was a living instrument of worship, crafted with glory and honor to lead the heavens in praise. But pride and lust for worship overtook him.

Violence and rebellion rose in his heart. He was cast down from heaven, and with him, a third of the angels.

Now, Satan lives to fill what God loves most—you and me—with what God hates most: rebellion. He is the accuser of the brethren, constantly seeking to drive us into shame, division, and darkness. He is a liar, the father of lies. He is not all-knowing, not all-powerful, not all-present.

He is a created being, and he knows the principles of the Kingdom better than many believers do. He knows this: we will become what we worship. If he can get us to behold him—to focus on his lies, his chaos, his nature—then we will begin to reflect that brokenness. Lust, impurity, violence, bitterness, pride, and greed are all symptoms of his fallen image. And the more we fix our gaze on these things, the more we reflect them.

"Whoever believes in Me, as scripture has said, rivers of living water will flow from within them" **(John 7:38).**

So, when we sit and behold the beauty of Jesus, the Lamb of God, we are filled with love, peace, joy, and power. We become whole. We become holy. We become living epistles, known and read by all men. We become ambassadors of the Kingdom of Heaven, carrying the divine nature into every place we go.

"The Son is the radiance of God's glory and the exact representation of his being, sustaining all things by his powerful word" **(Hebrews 1:3).**

This is why worship and obedience are not optional in the Kingdom—they are foundational. God is not looking for performance. He is looking for people who behold Him, because as we do, His nature flows into us and through us. We become a people of wisdom, a people who hear His voice, and a people who reflect His glory.

Obedience is Worship

"And we will be ready to punish every act of disobedience, once your obedience is complete" **(2 Corinthians 10:6).**

Our obedience brings heaven to earth, and every act of our obedience is a form of worship, and that worship is our warfare. And when we go and do what God asks us to do, no matter how big or small, God moves in so many directions, and heaven is released.

This type of worship shows all creation that God is "Worthy" of our "Worth ship Offering" of obedience, and that smashes the enemy straight in the mouth. This is war, and the way to win is to follow your leader, your King, as he did his Father, so we do now.

This is how much God is involved in our daily lives if we allow him to be, leading and guiding us through this world for a myriad of reasons and duties, and this is a form of worship when we obey. When we instantly trust and obey God and move when he leads us to move, even if it's some silly little act of faith.

For instance, driving for an hour in your car in one direction and then getting out to pray for a minute, then heading home - these moments of obedience can counteract the works of disobedience in the spiritual realm around you.

So, when God is nudging you to obey something small and insignificant, and it doesn't make sense, it is for your soul's sake to obey and move with Him, because He is setting you up for a victory. God is the one who is responsible for the growth of our faith, and we are responsible for responding, obeying, and following his word and his spirit.

To obey is better than sacrifice. Our obedience will open doors to adventures and encounters with God that will shape who you are and who God is in your eyes, helping to develop you as a well-rounded leader in the Kingdom.

God is looking to create leaders who fully express His nature and character, and these private moments of obedience lead to increased intimacy and capabilities in your life. It will serve to show you who he is experientially so that you can pass that on to this world.

We need leaders who have been touched by the Fire of God, shaped in His image in that Fire, filled with the Joy of the Lord, and leaders whose hearts burn brightly with God, who are, by doing, becoming more and more like Christ. When you fail, not if, but when you fail to obey, mercy is waiting, and you will have to deal with the pain and the sting of disobedience. However, you're a child, learning and growing.

God is always seeking to establish your life in Him, and the best way is through experience—stepping out of the norm and comfort. Learning to follow His leadings and promptings is how we understand His character. They are the same.

He is his nature, and his nature is him, goodness, kindness, self-control, and so on, so we will learn his will in his ways.

Great leadership includes temporary defeats; overcoming setbacks teaches problem-solving. Remember, Jesus learned obedience through suffering—perseverance and overcoming challenges help others find their way.

The Hidden Seasons of Growth: Embracing the Process

"It is the glory of God to conceal a matter; to search out a matter is the glory of kings" **(Proverbs 25:2).**

God rarely broadcasts His plans and purposes. Instead, we must exercise faith to trust that He remains in control. Each season of development contains exercises designed to sharpen and refine us, yet these tasks themselves are not the goal—the transformation they produce within us is the true objective.

Allowing God to work within us as we wait and embrace the process enables Him to shape us in unexpected ways. Reaching the mountain to be with Jesus and see His glory is the pinnacle, but the lessons are found in how we got there, in the strength of our stories. The mountain view is stunning, and it becomes even richer as we reflect on the path we took to reach it.

Some of our most significant transformations occur in complete solitude, witnessed only by ourselves and God. During these times of hiddenness, we learn to manage boredom, process complex emotions, and heal from loss. The lessons learned are often specifically for you and God alone.

People may eventually notice the fruits of this hidden work—perhaps in your increased patience, deeper wisdom, or greater compassion—without ever knowing the private struggles that produced them. They see the harvest but not the seasons of planting and tending that made it possible. And that's okay—there is a time for everything. These private moments of growth shape who we become, yet remain largely invisible to the outside world.

The internal victories over impatience, the gradual strengthening of resilience, the quiet surrender of pride—these profound changes transform us from within. Waiting is powerful when we surrender fully to it and trust God deeply during the process. We cannot rush to the end of a season or fast-track our development—we must submit to the timing and process God has ordained.

Times of submitting, learning, and waiting aren't passive periods but active opportunities for internal growth. There's wisdom in recognizing when it's time to step back rather than step forward. Throughout spiritual history, we see patterns of retreat and preparation before a significant calling or purpose is revealed.

As I began this current season, I started writing and compiling past writings for a book. Each day, I approached the work as if it were my job—writing, editing, carefully choosing words with the end reader in mind. I worked diligently, believing I was creating something that would take both myself and my readers somewhere meaningful, where together we would learn.

In the midst of this focused effort, I heard God's voice one morning while working at my desk: "Don't rush the process," He said gently but firmly. "Don't run ahead. Embrace the process." I paused, fingers hovering over the keyboard, and felt something shift inside. That moment marked a turning point—a glimpse of light at the end of the tunnel. I began to see more clearly what was happening in this season.

"Lord, is this about the book or about my life?" I asked.

"Both," came the reply. "I'm not just referencing your current life season but specifically the book itself and your writing process. Don't rush the development of this book. Don't be in a hurry. Don't rush what I am working IN YOU as you are working ON this project."

What a profound realization—that God was working on me as I worked on this book. The challenge is real. "I in you and you in me and we are in the Father," He reminded me. "I am working on you as you are working on this book."

Yes, the book would eventually be written and finished, but the process of writing it—the discipline of pressing through, doing the work, and learning how to create in this way—was God's primary work for me.

The book had become the tool God was using in this season of development. Through it, I learned about the process itself and how to push past my perceived limitations. The very act of writing had become both the means and the message.

What's remarkable is how the process of writing mirrored the message of the book itself: to endure, to embrace challenges, to persevere, to push through obstacles, and to lean on God throughout. The purpose of writing the book paralleled the experience of attending college—both are fundamentally about the process of learning, about development, and about being shaped for purposes greater than degrees or publications.

This season of writing has been about self-discovery and transcendence—learning about myself, growing beyond my limitations, and becoming more like Christ as He develops my character, readiness, trust, and faith. Do not rush the process you are in at this moment, and do not rush what is being developed in you. Focus on what God is growing in you during this season. Prioritize rest and obedience over striving. The more we yield and surrender, the easier it will be.
We usually never know what test God is preparing us for

before entering these seasons. And we rarely understand why until the season is over. Whether it be seasons of isolation or hiddenness, God seldom broadcasts them to us. If we knew the test ahead of time, we might avoid it or try to assist God in the process in ways we shouldn't.

However, you will get glimpses of the "what" and "why" when you find yourself sharing encouragement with someone in need. God provides moments of fellowship, where you speak from what is in your spirit, and as you speak, you realize how much you have just learned. You walk away encouraged.

These moments of transition occur for numerous reasons, such as the passing of the mantle between old and new leaders to usher in a new generation. Paul passed the baton to Timothy, Moses to Joshua, Elijah to Elisha, and, in one way, John to Jesus. We see fathers passing to sons, from generation to generation, and from epoch to epoch.

Some opposition is an indicator that the transition is happening—like the passing of the torch or baton from one runner to the next. There is always a little tension or opposition internally before the handoff. With mantles, we see the forerunner giving way to the pioneer, and the passing of the old to the new is an ongoing process in God's kingdom.

This is happening all around me—and TO me! I speak from a current position of waiting for the effective and favorable door to open, as I await a new season. I see open doors as "side missions" that happen in the meantime.

CHAPTER 14
LET GOD DO IT- SHALOM (WHOLENESS)

"He who began a good work for us, He will complete it"
(Philippians 1:6).

Our God is a complete God. He is a God of fullness and of finishing. He would never command us to do anything that He Himself would not do. He is a God of perfect character. Scripture tells us that finishing is better than starting, and this reveals His nature: He is faithful to complete what He begins.

"He who began a good work in you will carry it on to completion until the day of Christ Jesus" **(Philippians 1:6).**

You can count on Him, because He cannot lie. He will bring His work in you to fullness. He is a whole God, a full God, the God of Shalom—peace, wholeness, nothing lost, nothing broken, nothing incomplete. This is His grace and favor upon all who belong to Him.

The early church lived in this reality:

"And God's grace was so powerfully at work in them all that there were no needy persons among them" **(Acts 4:33-34).**

Grace is not only pardon—it is power. Mercy is forgiveness we do not deserve, but grace is the enabling power of God to live as forgiven people. Because of His grace, they lacked nothing: no strength, no provision, no direction. The same grace and shalom rest on you. The favor and anointing of God is upon you, making you complete in Him, lacking nothing. Yes, the enemy will try—through discord, division, and confusion—but our call is to remain vigilant. The great harvest is coming; it cannot be delayed much longer.

Our goal, as always, is to abide in Him with inward rest. This is our labor: to be still, to trust, not leaning on our own strength or understanding. To abide is the highest form of worship, for it testifies before the world and the devil where our true hope rests. Right now, God is preparing us. He is working with us. The key is to let Him finish what He started. He is making a way through the enemy's attacks and through every resistance that rises against us.

Those who receive the messenger will receive the message.Like Mary, when the angel Gabriel came—she saw the angel, she heard him, she believed him, and she received the message. Then she gave birth to the Messenger. Her cousin did the same. They both believed and received—and became.

They believed. They received. They became.

When we become the message, God comes to us and begins weaving into us what we will become. Not just as image-bearers or ambassadors, but as the living message He wants to speak to the world—through a surrendered life. He leads us beside still waters. We were created to be one with God, intimate with our Creator—from whom all life flows like a living stream. The headwaters of that river flow from His being into ours. And the doorway into that river is daily faith—a living, constant, ongoing relationship with Him.

Our daily delight in God produces, just as Scripture says, a desire to know Him, to be near Him, to follow Him. And more: desires to go, to become, to step into all He created us to be. He is always drawing us to Himself. As we pay attention, think, talk with Him, and invite Him into the moments and details of our lives—He shows up.

This is worship. True worship is living with God in mind and acting accordingly. It shows the world who He is.
Be a master of the moments in your life—recognize when Jesus is speaking, what He is doing, and when He is in the room. Be present in your relationships, in your business dealings, in your friendships. Be available—to people, to the moment, to what's happening around you. Pay attention.

Be present. But do it with God at the center of your thoughts. Let Him lead you in every interaction—not strangely or religiously, but in a way that leaves the door open for the Holy Spirit to move.

Leave room in every moment for God to give wisdom and insight. Become an executor of the moment—aware of what to say or not say, what to do or not do. What price to charge? What deal to make—or to walk away from? What promise to give. What commitment to keep. Be the kind of person who recognizes when God wants to interact with you or with others—in small or big ways. All we have to do is stay open, stay aware, and listen.

Practice His presence

Pay attention to how He partners with you—how He leads you to give good gifts, find the best deal, park in the right spot, or speak the right word. These things come as we allow God to be more. Staying in a prayerful state—aware that He is with us, listening to our thoughts even before we think them—positions us to live as His friend.

Most of my communication with God is inward and silent. Before I make decisions, sometimes He gives a leading.

Often, before I wake up, I sense He's already arranging my day. He orders our steps. He counts the hairs on our heads. He knows precisely when and where to lead.

This awareness is the wellspring of adventure and friendship. It is dynamic—alive with His presence and power. It's where we begin to know Him deeply. It's where He begins to share His heart and His desires. It's where we follow Him beside still waters into secret moments—sunrises, sunsets, whispers of love and clarity. He longs to share His secrets.

But He shares them only with those who will honor them. The noise of life—its circus, crowds, and endless motion—can distract both the learned and the broken, the rich and the wise. But the mysteries? They are beside the still waters, out of view. Set aside for the few who are willing to listen—who are ready for divine surprises, sacred whispers, and unexpected promotions.

To come away with God, to be with Him anywhere and at any time, is to discover the hidden treasures in the small moments: beauty, joy, and revelation. And your heart is filled with such fullness, and you become awed by His ability to master the moments of your life—even without your help.

These moments come for the few who will go to the unusual places, at the unusual times. For those willing to meet Him apart from the crowds. For those who can hear the whispers of the King. He is always calling us into the deep places of His heart. Israel knew God's deeds, but Moses knew God's ways. And you can too. You can know God's ways. You can know His heart. You can know God.

CONCLUSION:
THE CONCLUSION OF THE MATTER

"Now all has been heard; here is the conclusion of the matter: Fear God and keep his commandments, for this is the duty of all mankind. For God will bring every deed into judgment, including every hidden thing, whether it is good or evil"
(Ecclesiastes 12:13,14).

As we come to the end of this part of our journey together, I want to leave you with a simple truth: the pursuit of God is not a destination—it's an ongoing adventure. Each day brings new opportunities to know Him more deeply, to experience His presence more fully, and to become more like Him in every way.

This is the road less traveled—the narrow way. All are called to walk the road with Jesus, and all are called to have burning hearts. But very, very few choose it, and fewer still continue.

The dynamic relationship with God that we've explored in these pages is available to anyone who seeks Him with their whole heart. It doesn't require special talent, perfect behavior, or extraordinary circumstances. It simply requires your "yes"—a willingness to step out of the comfortable and familiar and into the wild and wonderful journey God has prepared for you.

It takes a heart surrendered daily, by faith. Not a faith focused on getting things, but a faith fixed on gaining a person—Jesus. It will take perseverance, grit, and a deep determination to honor God above yourself and above the approval of man.

You were created for this—to know God, and to be fully known by Him. Every longing in your heart, every question about your purpose, every desire for more—all these points back to the One who has placed eternity in your heart.

So, what will you do with this invitation?

Will you settle for a casual acquaintance with your Creator? Or will you pursue the deep, spirit-to-spirit intimacy He offers? Will you stay safely on the shore? Or will you step out into the deep waters of His love?

The choice is yours. But I pray you'll choose the adventure. I pray you'll give your "yes" to God—today and every day. I pray you'll cultivate the kind of relationship that transforms you from the inside out. And don't be in a hurry—to arrive, to perform, or to become some ideal version of a Christian, you think you should be.

Over time, as you walk with Him, you'll discover who God truly is—and in the process, you will find your most authentic self. Be who God made you to be. Do what you know He's calling you to do. Follow Him with one goal and one purpose: to be as close to His heart as you can be.

The world needs you—not a version of you, not a copy of someone else, but the original you God designed in your mother's womb. The real you—whole, healed, and sold out for Christ.

"For in Him we live and move and have our being" **(Acts 17:28).**

As you continue your journey, remember that you're not alone. Not only is God with you every step, but you're also surrounded by a family of fellow travelers—those who have gone before you, those walking with you now, and those who will follow in your footsteps.

May you discover the joy of knowing God more deeply than you ever imagined. May you experience the freedom that comes from surrendering fully to His love. May you become so filled with His presence that it overflows to everyone around you.

"The only thing that truly matters is faith expressed through love" **(Galatians 5:6).**

Three weeks after I was saved and delivered, my friend Ken Freebairn said to me, in his blunt, brotherly way: "Rick, calm down, wild man. Just love God, love people, hate sin, and walk in power toward the devil."

"Now to Him who is able to keep you from stumbling and to present you blameless before the presence of His glory with great joy" **(Jude 1:24).**

You didn't save yourself, and you can't keep yourself. It is Christ in you who does all the work because true Christianity is from the inside out, not the outside in.

It is a life transformed by the power of God, not by the willpower of men. That was the mystery hidden for ages but revealed to us all by God for us today.

"Christ in you, the hope of glory" **(Colossians 1:27).**

So, keep burning, my friends. Stay hungry, stay thirsty, and stay in the river of God. Above all else, be bold, be brave, and let Jesus live big inside you.

With all Christ's Love, Thanks for stopping by.

MAY YOUR JOURNEY WITH GOD BEGIN!

Notes

Notes

www.ingramcontent.com/pod-product-compliance
Lightning Source LLC
Chambersburg PA
CBHW011319080526
44589CB00018B/2733